TRUE AND ?

Weird Stories from the World's Newswires

MONICA HOOSE & CAROLYN NAIFEH

Illustrations by Keith Johnston

TOPPER BOOKS
AN IMPRINT OF PHAROS BOOKS • A SCRIPPS HOWARD COMPANY
NEW YORK

For our parents
George and Marion Naifeh
Bill and Dorothy Hoose

The material in this book has been reprinted with the permission of the Agence France Presse, the Associated Press, Reuters Information Services, and United Press International.

Copyright © 1990 by Monica Hoose and Carolyn Naifeh.
Illustrations copyright © Pharos Books.
All rights reserved. No part of this book may be reproduced in any form or by any means without written permission of the publisher.

First published in 1990.

Printed in the United States of America.

Topper Books
An Imprint of Pharos Books
A Scripps Howard Company
200 Park Avenue
New York, N.Y. 10166

10 9 8 7 6 5 4 3 2 1

Pharos Books are available at special discounts on bulk purchases for sales promotions, premiums, fundraising or educational use. For details, contact the Special Sales Department, Pharos Books, 200 Park Avenue, New York, NY 10166

Acknowledgments

We are especially grateful for the advice of our agent, Mel Berger, as well as to Steve Naifeh and Fran Lebowitz, who pitched in whenever we needed a helping hand. Lori Gilliam with UPI, Tom Slaughter with AP, Brian Williams with Reuters and Georges Deschodt and Herve Couturier with AFP were always generous with their time. A special thanks to Steve Beckner, Niki Butler, Bob Dore, Sally Hodgson, Ravi M. Khanna, Mollie King, Neils Lindquist, Andrew Miga and John O'Rourke for their help. And, finally, we'd like to thank our editor at Pharos Books, Shari Jee, who was always there for us.

Contents

Make a Date with a Great Psychoanalyst	**9**
Different Strokes	**17**
To Catch a Thief	**25**
Oops!	**41**
Tom, Dick and Hairy	**49**
Stupid Human Tricks	**55**
It Came in Through the Bathroom Window	**67**

Wild Kingdom	**71**
Man Bites Dog	**83**
Finger Lickin' Good	**89**
Fifty Ways to Leave Your Lover	**97**
Easy Rider	**103**
Business Is Business	**111**
Birds Do It, Bees Do It	**119**

Introduction

"The lovely woman-child Kaa was mercilessly chained to the cruel post of the warrior-chief beastx, with his barbarian tribe now stacking wood at her nubile feet, when the strong clear voice of the poetic and heroic Handsomas roared, 'Flick your bic, crisp that chick, and you'll feel my steel through your last meal.'"

—Steve Garman's winning entry in the San Jose State Bulwer-Lytton contest that seeks the opening sentence to the worst of all possible novels.

Make a Date with a Great Psychoanalyst

Pole Breaks Own Record

WARSAW, POLAND (Reuters) A Pole has broken his own world record by bouncing a tennis ball on his head for an hour and 45 minutes—17 minutes longer than his previous best. Janusz Chomatek bounced the ball on his head 15,225 times at a rate of 145 times a minute, the newspaper *Dziennik Ludowy* said Friday. It did not say when he set the record.

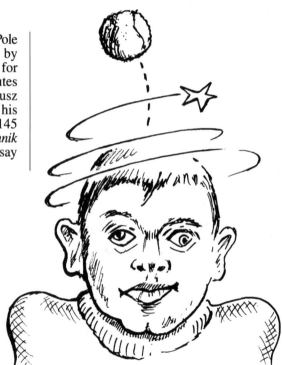

Contractor Undrills Steel Shaft from Skull

TORONTO (UPI) Donald Wright said Wednesday that restarting a power drill to pull three inches of steel out of his skull had nothing to do with courage—he just wanted to stay alive.

Wright, a 54-year-old Toronto contractor, was working on a ladder last Wednesday when he toppled onto a 3/8-inch drill bit that was pointing upwards.

He passed out but regained consciousness and realized the drill bit was stuck in his skull.

Instead of phoning for an ambulance, Wright decided he would attempt to remove the bit himself and get out of the locked apartment so someone could find him in case he passed out again.

"I passed out; then when I came to, I felt like I was having seizures. I was feeling icy cold all over and I just couldn't move myself," Wright said from his hospital bed.

"When I was trying to move, it was like my head was nailed to the floor and it was because the drill was holding me down."

He got up after six attempts and, holding the five-pound drill level with the angle that the drill entered the right side of his skull around the hairline, he went to the bathroom with the extension cord dragging behind him.

"I was worried about my brain because I had this drill sticking in my head," Wright said. "There was no pain, but my body was numb and I was frightened my bodily senses had been killed.

"I tried to pull it out but it wouldn't come out. So I knew the only way to get it out was by restarting it.

"I looked into the mirror and I restarted the drill and pulled it out of my head," he said. Blood spurted from the wound. "I thought my brains were pouring out with the blood. But I felt no pain."

Wright was in the apartment, four floors below his own in downtown Toronto, to install a sliding door. Fearing he might pass out again, he left the apartment, locked the door behind him and took the elevator to his own apartment.

He was leaving for the hospital when his wife returned home, called an ambulance and rushed him to nearby Wellesley Hospital.

Researcher Bitten by Snake for 148th Time

SALT LAKE CITY (AP) A 78-year-old snake-venom researcher was in serious but stable condition today after suffering his 148th snake bite, that of a venomous Pakistani pit viper.

William E. Haast, who assumed he was immune to the viper, waited about 24 hours after the bite before checking himself into the University of Utah Health Sciences Center on Wednesday.

He was treated with massive doses of antivenin, including a shipment obtained through an unusual airport relay involving a California zoo, a helicopter and a departing jetliner.

"He was and is a very sick man and needs the antivenin. Apparently, he gets massive doses of it," said John Dwan, hospital spokesman.

"In addition, they're giving him parts of blood that the venom has destroyed. They're trying to rebuild his blood coagulation ability by countering the venom and building up his own blood," Dwan said.

Doctors had been unable to give him antivenin immediately because he had built up an allergic reaction to the stock on hand during previous snake bites.

A regional poison control center in Albuquerque, New Mexico, was contacted and the appropriate antivenin was located at the San Diego Zoo.

A batch of it arrived on a Delta Air Lines flight about 7 p.m. Wednesday. A second shipment was dispatched later aboard an America West flight, put on the plane at the last minute at Lindbergh Field in San Diego.

The plane was approaching the runway for takeoff when the airline was notified of the emergency shipment, said America West spokeswoman Daphne Dicino.

At first, officials feared it was too late to get the package on the plane, but the pilot offered over the radio to accept it. A helicopter that had picked up the shipment from the zoo landed nearby and the package was handed to the pilot through the cockpit window.

Haast, director of Miami Serpentarium Laboratories at the university's Research Park, maintains 1,000 exotic, poisonous snakes at the lab, which provides venom to health organizations and others for research and use in manufacturing antivenins.

Suicide Bid Succeeds on Second Attempt

BARCELONA, SPAIN (Reuters) A 44-year-old man plunged to his death from a third-story balcony after a passerby thwarted his first try by cushioning his fall, police said today.

Both were unhurt in the first attempt yesterday, but the intended suicide went back to his apartment for a second, successful jump, police said.

Bone-Clad "Prince" Makes a Case for Freedom of Dress

MEMPHIS, TENN. (AP) A Criminal Court judge has ruled that a defendant can't show up for trial wearing fur, bones, goggles and green body paint—even if he is a native of the planet Zambodia.

But an attorney for the man who calls himself Prince Mongo wants to make a federal case out of his client's 10-day jail sentence for contempt of court.

Judge Odell Horton of U.S. District Court was scheduled to decide the issue today in Mongo's appeal of a contempt order by Judge William Williams.

The dispute began when Robert Hodges appeared before Williams on a charge of tampering with an electric meter.

Hodges, who says he is really Prince Mongo from Zambodia, was not wearing the suit and tie customary for trial defendants.

In the judge's contempt of court citation, he said the defendant "appeared for trial dressed in a grossly shocking and bizarre attire, consisting of brown and white fur tied around his body at his ankles, loins and head, with a like vest made out of the fur, and complete with eye goggles over his eyes.

"He had colored his face and chest with a very pale green paint or coloring. He had what appeared to be a human skull dangling from his waist and in his hand he carried a stuffed snake."

Hodges, who gives his age as 3,000 and who once ran for Shelby County mayor, has often been at odds with his neighbors and city officials, usually because of his unusual taste in landscaping.

He once appeared barefoot and in a fur coat before a U.S. District Court judge and scattered an unidentified powder before the bench to ward off what he called "spirits." That was during a lawsuit against two insurance companies that refused to pay him disability benefits after he said he was mentally impaired.

He won the suit.

Loan

WASHINGTON (UPI) A robed man calling himself King A.A. Zodiac XV caused a stir at a bank across the street from the Treasury Department by asking for a $900,000 loan, the FBI said.

The man, carrying a shepherd's staff, walked into the Riggs National Bank Monday and asked to borrow the money "for religious purposes," a Federal Bureau of Investigations spokesman said.

Suspicious bank officials called the FBI to interview the man, but the federal agents determined Zodiac had committed no crime and they left the scene, the spokesman said. The man was turned down for the loan.

The bank is located on busy Pennsylvania Avenue, across from the Treasury Department and not far from the White House. Scores of homeless people, including many former mental patients, are known to frequent the parks in the area.

A bank spokesman said, "The incident ended with no actions being taken against anyone." An FBI agent joked that Zodiac "parted Pennsylvania Avenue" when he left the bank.

Nuisance

CHATTANOOGA, TENN. (UPI) Gertrude Jamieson, an 85-year-old woman who harassed a man with crank phone calls for 43 years, was spared a possible second term as a prisoner Friday because prosecutors feared she might die in the workhouse.

"We're not going to put an old lady who's dying in jail," Assistant District Attorney Jerry Sloan said. "It's our understanding that her health is deteriorating."

Hamilton County Criminal Court Judge Russell Hinson was to consider sending Mrs. Jamieson to the penal farm for 11 months and 25 days—a sentence that was suspended last year when she took an oath to stop the harassing calls to A. Douglas Thompson.

Thompson, 59, filed a new complaint in January, alleging the calls had resumed.

But Assistant District Attorney Jerry Sloan agreed to dismiss the complaint after Mrs. Jamieson's attorney said his feeble client is bedridden and confined to a nursing home in a room without a phone.

Sloan said Mrs. Jamieson could not be cared for at the penal farm and might die there.

"She's a rough pill to get along with."

"Mrs. Jamieson had a stroke and broke her hip. She's in a room now with no phone, and unless she can get one of the attendants to wheel her down the hall, the calls will stop," said Mickey Barker, Mrs. Jamieson's lawyer.

Mrs. Jamieson, who spent four months at the Hamilton County penal farm in 1965 for making the harassing calls, has been charged dozens of times by Thompson, who said his phone rang up to 20 times a day over the decades.

Thompson incurred the wrath of Mrs. Jamieson in 1940 when he was a 16-year-old newspaper delivery boy and Mrs. Jamieson's shaggy white dog leaped from hedges and nipped him on the heel.

Thompson said he had the canine caged at the city pound and Mrs. Jamieson never forgot, even though the dog was returned to her a few days later.

"She's a rough pill to get along with," Thompson said. "She's just mean as the devil."

Different Strokes

Tickle

MINEOLA, N.Y. (UPI) A 20-year-old Long Island man was under arrest Monday, charged with sneaking into the home of two young women, tickling their feet and stealing their shoes.

The man is also a suspect in five similar incidents since last September—all involving tickling women's feet, police said.

"In my 28 years on the force, I have never encountered a case like this," said Nassau County Detective Louis Fucito. "I rather think that this young man needs some medical attention."

Richard Hunter, 20, of Roslyn Heights, was arrested at his home Sunday and charged with two counts of second-degree burglary. His father, the Rev. Richard Hunter, is pastor of the Friendship Baptist Church in Roslyn Heights.

Fucito said Hunter entered a house in Roslyn Heights at 4 a.m. May 24 and sneaked into the bedroom of Oyra Ostad, 15, where he tickled her feet, awakening her.

> "This young man needs some medical attention."

When the girl screamed, he grabbed one of her shoes and fled.

On June 18, he returned to the same home at 4:30 a.m., invaded the bedroom of Oyra's sister, Fariba, 21, and tickled her feet. When she cried out, Hunter ran off with three of her shoes, Fucito said.

The suspect was arrested on June 8 on a trespassing charge after he had ignored repeated warnings to stay away from the Roslyn High School campus because he was not a student there, Fucito said.

Man Detained, Accused of Biting the Buttocks of Dozens of Women

PUNTA ARENAS, CHILE (UPI) A man, 23, was arrested in this southern city, accused of biting the buttocks of dozens of women, police said.

Jorge Delgado Andrade, nicknamed by the local papers as the "Dog Man," will be prosecuted on charges of causing his victims physical injury and violating public decency, said police.

According to police, Delgado began his attacks last August, when he bit the buttocks of an 18-year-old girl as she was walking down a suburban street in Punta Arenas.

Later, he attacked a number of women who were walking alone in the city, which is located on the banks of the Magallanes, 2,000 kilometers south of Santiago.

Police believe there are other victims of the "Dog Man" who did not report the attacks, but who might come forward now that he is in prison.

Footstomper Steps Out of Line Again

NASHVILLE, TENN. (UPI) George "Footstomper" Mitchell, whose brutal attraction to the female instep has earned him national notoriety and years in jail, has done it again.

Mitchell had been out of prison less than a month Sunday when his urge to stomp on women's insteps came over him.

He put on his three-piece black pinstripe suit, inserted a rose in the lapel, pulled on his wooden-heeled black dress shoes, strolled down to the bus station and ran amok.

Before it was over, said metro police Detective John Patton, "Footstomper" had stomped on the insteps of three women. The victims "hobbled around when they left," Patton said, "but none required medical treatment."

Mitchell was charged with four counts of aggravated assault, including assaulting the officer who arrested him.

He pulled on his wooden-heeled black dress shoes ... and ran amok.

He was released less than a month ago from a minimum-security prison where he was serving a four-year term for stomping on women's feet. During the past fifteen years, Mitchell has been arrested more than forty times for stomping. He has spent all but eight months of the past thirteen years in jail.

"I'm not really no bad person, but it seems like something just takes over, an urge or something, and I can't do nothing about it," Mitchell testified in 1981.

"It sounds funny at first, but I'll bet you that habit of his is going to wind up killing him," Patton said.

"One day he's going to stomp one too many. One day he's going to pull that stunt on somebody's wife when her husband is standing nearby, and he's going to kill him. I would if he stomped on my wife's feet," Patton said.

Exorcism

BANGKOK, THAILAND (UPI) Buddhist monks sprinkled holy water and Chinese dragon dancers pranced at a dangerous Bangkok intersection to exorcise spirits of traffic accident victims, newspapers reported Wednesday.

Nine saffron-robed monks chanted and sprinkled holy water on the pavement Tuesday following complaints that the spirits of dead accident victims were causing nightmares for people living near the intersection, the reports said.

The religious rite, a Chinese dragon dance and the burning of symbolic gold- and silver-colored papers, stopped traffic at the busy junction of Rama IV and Saphan Lueng roads.

But instead of honking horns or complaining about the stalled traffic, motorists bowed reverently and prayed for the mercy of the traffic spirits.

No-Toad-Licking Zone

COLUMBIA, SOUTH CAROLINA (AP) Worried that his constituents might lick or kiss a South American toad to get at the hallucinogenic toxin it secretes, a legislator has introduced a bill making it illegal to get high on cane toads.

"It's the latest wave" in hallucinating, said Rep. Pat Harris, citing the Drug Enforcement Administration's recent toad-licking alert.

Harris said Thursday he has not heard of instances of cane toad-licking in South Carolina, although he said it was potentially an explosive phenomenon. "Crack could pale" in significance, he joked.

"They say these frogs grow to the size of a dinner plate. I don't want to see somebody walk across the State-

house grounds with a frog on a leash and pick him up and lick him."

Harris admitted his bill was good for nothing more than [a] laugh.

"It's a kind of tongue-in-cheek deal," the 78-year-old real estate executive said. "Kind of tongue-on-the-frog deal."

Cane toads, endemic to South America, produce a toxin called bufotenine to ward off predators. When licked raw, or cooked, the toxin acts as a hallucinogen.

Asked if he would consider kissing a cane toad to hallucinate, Harris replied, "Oh no, no. No. I'd rather drink a lot of liquor."

Feathers to Feathers: Max the Parrot Gets Full Funeral Service

SANTA CLARA, CALIF. (AP) About 20 relatives and friends who gathered at the funeral of 5-year-old Max remembered him as an ordinary fellow who enjoyed a steamy morning shower.

The departed was actually a feathered friend—an African gray parrot.

"There's no replacement for Max," said Robin Patterson, 26, of Santa Clara. "He'd shower with me in the morning. He'd sit with me if I was sick. If he did something bad, he'd turn around and say, 'What are ya doing?' "

Capt. A.G. Maximilian Cricket was remembered Tuesday in a service at the First Presbyterian Church of Santa Clara. He died in Patterson's arms Sunday, three days after he was smashed in a car door.

The Rev. Wayne Faust, who conducted the service, admitted he'd never done anything like it before, "only for my kids' pets in the backyard."

"But to Robin, Max was a friend and part of their family. His death was very traumatic."

Fired from Rolls Royce for Dangerous Hair

BRISTOL, ENGLAND (AP) An 18-year-old punk rocker, fired by Rolls Royce on grounds that the four-inch spikes of his hairdo endangered the eyes of his co-workers, lost an appeal against the decision Tuesday.

Peter Mortiboy, whose unusual dress including 18 earrings, a studded dog collar, steel armlets and a stud through his nose, was repeatedly warned by Rolls that his appearance was not up to company standards, an industrial tribunal in this west coast port was told.

The luxury car maker dismissed him from the Rolls Royce Technical College and his $120-a-week job as an apprentice technician when he began sporting spikes last June, training manager Howard Parry testified.

"His hairstyle represented a safety hazard," Parry said. "The spikes

projected from the surface of his head for some distance and an accidental movement could have injured a supervisor leaning over him.

Mortiboy, who said he used industrial adhesive and glue to mold his black hair into stiff, vertical spikes, denied that the spikes are dangerous.

"They would be if they were three feet long," he said. "I mix with people all the time in crowded nightclubs and I have never injured anyone," he said. "I didn't cut them off because I'm not happy unless I look the way I want to look... The only trouble I have is sleeping. I have to lie on my stomach."

To Catch a Thief

Pigeon Thief

BALTIMORE, MARYLAND (AP) A Baltimore man has been arrested for stealing 70 homing pigeons. Police say about a third of them were discovered alive, inside his pants.

They say they caught Thomas Waddell when they saw him walking strangely—with bulging pants.

One police officer says, "He looked like the Michelin tire ad."

The officer says as he approached Waddell, the suspect was stuffing a pigeon down his pants.

After Waddell was arrested, the officer says, he began shaking and pulling pigeons from his pants. In all, police say, he pulled out 21 live pigeons and five dead ones.

Waddell is accused of stealing the pigeons from two other Baltimore men. He's charged with grand theft—and with cruelty to animals.

Hamburglars

CANONSBURG, PA (AP) A statue of Ronald McDonald, the smiling, red-mopped clown, was "abducted" from outside a fast-food restaurant and held ransom for 150 hamburgers, 150 milkshakes and one diet soda—all to go.

Police said the handwritten ransom note, slipped through a slot in the drive-in window, was signed "The Hamburglar," a character featured in McDonald's advertising.

The note warned that the statue would be dismembered, melted into ashtrays and donated to a roast beef restaurant if the conditions were not met, authorities said.

Samuel McClain, 22, and Carmine D'Amico, 21, both of Canonsburg, were arrested by police early Wednesday after an officer allegedly spotted the life-size, fiberglass statue in their car.

"There was no place they could hide him," a policeman said.

Police said the two would be arraigned today.

"It was just a prank by a couple of kids out to have fun," Dan Cooper, assistant restaurant manager, said Wednesday night. "They didn't realize what kind of trouble they could get into."

150 hamburgers, 150 milkshakes and one diet soda

The statue was removed about 2:30 a.m. Wednesday from the restaurant's playground on Bobby Vinton Boulevard, named for the singer who hails from this Washington County town. The restaurant was closed at the time.

Police theorized the suspects used a hacksaw to slice through bolts beneath the statue's feet.

The ransom note said the statue would be returned in exchange for 150 quarter-pound hamburgers, 150 milkshakes, 1 Tab soft drink, and 150 Atari game cards, police said. The loot was to be left under the sliding board at the fenced-in playground today.

Police apprehended the suspects after they allegedly were spotted leaving the parking lot.

The statue, and its base, were valued at $2,000, police said.

Repeat Offense

CHICAGO (UPI) A bank robber with a fondness for familiar places was arrested after reintroducing himself to a teller he robbed last December and passing her a used holdup note.

The robber, who police believe staged three robberies at the same bank in the past two years, was arrested Wednesday.

"Remember me?"

He walked into the main branch of the Harris Trust & Savings Bank shortly after noon, past a security guard who was studying a bank camera photograph of a man who vanished with $26,400 last December 29th, said Police Capt. Frank J. Stack.

The robber approached the teller robbed in the Dec. 29th holdup. He handed her the same note used in the previous robbery, which read: "Please no trouble. Give me all your 100s, 50s and 20s."

Lt. John Skelly said the bandit even asked the teller, "Do you remember me?"

The teller sounded an alarm and police arrested Clyde J. Copeland, 25, of Chicago.

Snowcones

METAIRIE, LA. (UPI) A bandit who wheeled his bicycle to a snowcone stand, pulled out a pistol and robbed a 14-year-old girl of $32.90 has been sentenced to 99 years in prison and faces more than 200 years behind bars.

Tyrone Jack of Metairie received the maximum sentence for armed robbery under state law after being convicted of the August theft, authorities said Friday.

Officials said they may try to up the sentence because of a prior Jefferson Parish burglary conviction.

James Maxwell, Parish Assistant District Attorney, said the state will also try to determine if Jack, 20, has a prior felony conviction as a juvenile in Chicago, which could push his maximum sentence well beyond 200 years.

Keli Jackson, 14, testified during the trial she was working alone at the stand when Jack appeared on a bicycle, pulled a gun and demanded money.

Man Becomes Stuck in Ex-Wife's Chimney

JONES, OKLA. (AP) A man who was prowling at his ex-wife's house spent the night in her chimney and had inhaled so much soot he was unable to thank his rescuers Tuesday, authorities said.

"This is the first time I've ever worked [with] someone overdosing on soot," said Oklahoma County Undersheriff Jerry Biggers.

The man, whose name was not immediately released, was discovered inside the chimney about 10:30 a.m., but authorities believe he had been there since about 11 p.m. Monday, when the occupant of the house called about a prowler.

The man apparently had been trying to get into the home through the chimney and became stuck, said Sid Stell, a spokesman for the Midwest City Police Department.

The man, who was left temporarily speechless by the ordeal, was taken to a Midwest City hospital complaining of chest pains.

Button Bandit

WHARNCLIFF, W.VA. (AP) A thief has left 53-year old Joe Toler at loose ends.

Toler, a construction worker, says someone broke into his home sometime last week and carefully removed all of the buttons from his 40 sport coats and vests.

Toler said Tuesday that he became aware of the burglary when he noticed that a roll of 25 silver dollars was missing from his house.

It wasn't until later, when Toler grabbed a sport coat to wear to church, that he realized the extent of the theft, he said.

The threads holding each button had been severed with a knife or other sharp object, he said. None of the buttons from his wife's clothes was missing.

Toler said he doesn't know who would want his buttons, or why.

A spokeswoman for the Mingo County sheriff's department confirmed that the incident had been reported, but said police had no leads.

Toler's wife, Hazel, called the crime "weird."

It wasn't until later... that he realized the extent of the theft.

"People know my husband likes to dress well, and it must be somebody who wanted to get at him somehow. It must be somebody with a warped mind," she said.

"It had to be someone doped up, or a member of a cult or someone who is demon-possessed," Toler added.

Thieves Cook Fast Food

PARKERSBURG, W.VA. (AP) — Thieves looking for a midnight snack broke into a fast-food restaurant, fired up the grill and cooked up batches of hamburgers and french fries before leaving.

"I've never heard of anything like this happening in our chain before," said Dee Murphy, a shift manager at the Wendy's restaurant.

Thieves apparently broke the drive-in window and crawled into the restaurant early Thursday.

"They didn't take any money or anything like that," Police Chief Russ Miller said. "They cooked up some items and messed the place up somewhat, but it looks like they primarily went in there for the food."

Store employees noticed several hamburgers and fries were taken out of stock and cooked, Ms. Murphy said. The bun warmer also was turned on and several buns were missing.

Scared Robber

PITTSBURGH (AP) A gas station robbery went awry early Wednesday when the bandit accidentally fired his pistol into his pants, police said.

A gunman entered a gas station and demanded money, then put his pistol into his belt, police said. The weapon fired and the man screamed and ran away, police said.

A bullet was found in the floor and it was not known if the bandit was wounded, police said. No money was taken.

Robbery Suspect Caught on Fence with Pants Down

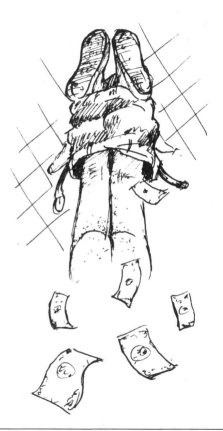

NEW YORK CITY (Reuters) The New York City police captured a robbery suspect who, frankly, didn't stand a chance of escape.

Police said the man was apprehended by 20 policemen with their guns drawn as he hung upside down from a fence Thursday in the backyard of a police station in Harlem with his pants at his ankles.

The man was wanted after allegedly stealing $200 from a nearby grocery store with another man who was caught in a more conventional manner— on a street corner.

The suspect apparently tried to jump the fence to elude police but got caught on it instead, police said.

Girdle Bust

HOUSTON (AP) The full-figured look just didn't suit a woman who arrived on a flight from Guatemala, and federal agents found she was wearing four girdles stuffed with cocaine.

U.S. Customs Service agents detained the 38-year-old Colombian woman Monday while she stood in line for a baggage search at Houston Intercontinental Airport.

"An agent noticed she was very nervous and that she was wearing very bulky clothing," said Candace Vice, chief customs inspector at the airport.

"We continued the inspection and discovered 16.3 pounds of cocaine secreted inside four girdles she was wearing," Ms. Vice said.

She said the woman was holding a ticket for a flight from Houston to Amsterdam.

"She was apparently heading to Holland because the value of cocaine is much greater there," she said. The cocaine would have been worth about three times more than the estimated $92,000 it would fetch in the United States, she said.

Man Arrested in Armed Robbery of a Beer

TULSA, OKLAHOMA (AP) A man who told a store clerk he had had a bad day pulled a .357-caliber Magnum handgun and stole a single bottle of beer, police said.

Police later arrested a man who handed over a gun but drank the rest of the evidence as officers approached.

A man took a 16-ounce bottle of beer to the counter of a convenience store Tuesday night, said Sgt. John Bowman.

"He said, 'Let me have this. I've had a bad day,'" Bowman said. "The attendant said he couldn't do that."

Bowman said the man then pulled the gun and pointed it at the clerk.

"He said, 'This is all I want. I don't want anything else,' and walked out the door while continuing to hold the gun on the attendant," Bowman said.

Officers later saw a man fitting the robber's description at a parking lot. Bowman said the officers approached the man and ordered him to drop the gun and the beer.

"I've had a bad day."

"He complied with half of the order and drank the rest of his beer," Bowman said.

Police jailed a 33-year-old Tulsa man pending the filing of formal charges.

Lottery "Winners" Find Their Prize Is Night in Jail

LOS ANGELES, CALIFORNIA (Reuters) More than 200 people who had been told they were winners in a lottery drawing turned up to collect their money only to find their prize was free accommodations—in the local jail.

"You're a big winner," police said one man was told at the Friday sting. "Have you any plans for tonight?" When he replied no, the jovial questioner said, "Don't worry, we'll take care of that."

The man, a probation violator, was led inside a building where, instead of the winnings he anticipated, he was awarded a pair of Los Angeles County Sheriff's Department handcuffs, firmly strapped around his wrists.

He was one of more than 500 people wanted by the department for various crimes who had failed to show up for their day in court.

The police lured 200 of the wanted people by mailing them letters saying they were big winners in a market survey company's test program for the California state lottery, and saying they could collect their cash prizes by turning up at a certain location Friday.

The "sting" operation went so well that some of the victims still wanted to know after their arrests if they could collect their winnings, a sheriff's deputy said.

Legalese

PORTLAND, MAINE (AP) It don't make no difference if prosecutors go after criminals with indictments that use bad grammar, the state's highest court said in a ruling that may help perpetuate generations of language abuse by lawyers.

Convicted arsonist Leon Corson, Sr., said he should have been cleared because the indictment against him was so poorly written and ambiguous that it made no sense.

The indictment returned by grand jurors in Piscataquis County contained a 180-word sentence that takes up 14 lines on the page. It said in part, that "with the intent that conduct be performed which, in fact, would constitute a crime or crimes," the fire in question was set.

The Maine Supreme Judicial Court's five justices did not buy Corson's arguments, saying the indictment, "even though grammatically incorrect, adequately informs the defenfant of the nature of the charge against him."

This week's ruling came as no surprise to scholars of English, who said lawyers are among the worst language offenders.

"A 180-word sentence should be taken out and shot."

"A 180-word sentence should be taken out and shot," said Richard Lederer, a columnist and language author from Concord, N.H. "It is disgraceful. They're trying to protect somebody's rights, and it's very tough to do with a 180-word sentence, even if it's 180 simple words."

The justices didn't see it that way, although they pointed out that Maine law insists an indictment "shall be a plain, concise and definite written statement of the essential facts constituting the offense charged."

That may well be too much to ask of lawyers.

They often use complex sentences decorated with such phrases as "to wit," "whereas," and "aforementioned," as well as numerous bits of Latin, in an attempt to show they are a special, educated class of people, scholars say.

"They won't call a spade a spade," Lederer said. "They call it an excavation device. It sometimes sounds more important."

Anyone who winds up being indicted with such confusing language can always get it translated into regular English, but the translation will come from yet another lawyer," he said.

Car Thief's Unusual Sentence

PLEASANTON, CALIF. (AP) A car thief spent the weekend in jail completing a sentence. Actually, 10,000 or so sentences.

Timothy Loggins, 20, had been ordered to write "If I don't own it, I won't take it" 10,000 times.

"I want him to feel that his repetitive writing is about as foolish as what he did," said Municipal Judge D. Ronald Hyde. "I want people to know that if you steal, you're going to pay a price, and it isn't always jail."

Loggins was released Monday after producing a thick batch of yellow, legal-size paper. The judge's clerk, Beverly Delucchi, said the last few hundred lines appeared to be written in a hand suffering from writer's cramp.

Asked if the judge counted the sentences, Delucchi said, "'I don't know. I know I didn't."

Loggins pleaded guilty last year, and Hyde sentenced him to five weekends in jail and ordered him to write the sentence as part of his probation. The judge jailed Loggins after learning he had not done his homework.

He Pleads Guilty; Jury Says He's Innocent

RICHMOND, VIRGINIA (UPI) A man charged with murdering an insurance agent switched his plea to guilty Wednesday only minutes before a jury voted to acquit him.

While the jury was deliberating for four and one-half hours Wednesday, Harry Seigler, his lawyers and prosecutors worked out a plea bargain agreement that included Seigler pleading guilty to a lesser charge and receiving a 60-year sentence with 20 years suspended.

Seigler, of Richmond, had pleaded innocent to the capital murder of insurance agent Douglas Mitchell, who was found with his throat slashed. Seigler could have received the death penalty if convicted of capital murder, but the charge was reduced to first-degree murder in the plea bargain.

The lawyers presented their plan to Richmond Circuit Judge William Spain, who asked Seigler if he was pleading guilty because he was guilty.

"Yes, sir," said Seigler.

"Holy mackerel."

Seigler was taken from the courtroom and the jury was allowed to enter. When informed of Seigler's reversal, one juror slumped in a chair and another bolted upright in his seat.

Examination of the jury's verdict form showed they were going to find Seigler innocent.

Seigler's lawyers, Thomas Gordon and John Dodson, said their client accepted the plea bargain because of concern for his mother's heart condition and because of the length of time the jury had deliberated.

When informed of the jury's vote, Dodson said, "Well, that's the risk you take."

Assistant Commonwealth's Attorney Warren Von Schuch said he had a feeling his case was in trouble and that was why he entered into the plea bargain agreement. When told of the jury's decision, Von Schuch said, "Holy mackerel."

Home, James...Fast

FRESNO, CALIFORNIA (UPI) Police had little trouble picking up the trail of a suspected bank robber, capturing him fleeing in a rented chauffeur-driven, black limousine.

It was the second time Gary Riley used a limousine as a getaway car, police said.

In the latest heist Wednesday, employees of Home Federal Savings gave police a description of the getaway sedan and officers stopped the Cadillac limousine on a freeway. They apprehended Riley, 25, and [the] driver, Shane Hite, without incident.

Police said they recovered an undisclosed amount of cash taken in the holdup and a pistol the robber used to force a teller to give the loot.

Detectives said they released driver Shane Hite because he knew nothing of the robbery. They said Hiley used a limousine to rob another bank May 31.

Oops!

Cracker Jacks

HUNTINGTON, W.VA. (UPI) An 8-year-old girl's surprise in a box of Cracker Jack was a booklet titled "Erotic Sexual Positions from Around the World," the girl's relatives say.

A spokeswoman for Borden Inc., maker of Cracker Jack, said Monday similar books were found in five boxes in other cities several month ago.

The booklet is a little more than an inch square and has several pages showing detailed drawings of people in various sex acts and positions. The cover states it is the first of a series of "erotic best sellers."

The grandmother of the Huntington girl who found the book said the child's "eyes got great big," and added, "She thought it was an exercise book."

Betty Garrett, a spokeswoman for Borden, based in Columbus, Ohio, attributed the books to "an individu-

al with a very sick sense of humor."

She said the books were put into the boxes during production and before being distributed.

The company has taken "intense steps to beef up security," including spot checks of the more than 300 million Cracker Jack boxes produced each year, she said.

"We have increased our security at every point that it could possibly be put into the system," Ms. Garrett said. "We really believe we have stopped it."

There's a Girl in My Soap

JACKSON, MISS. (UPI) Somebody pressed a wrong button and soap opera viewers got a glimpse of a nude woman, right in the middle of "Another World."

The picture popped up on the screen, temporarily interrupting "Another World."

Officials at WLBT Television station said Friday the photograph from *Playboy* Magazine was flashed on the screen Thursday in what was described as an "electronic typo."

"WLBT apologizes for this miscalculation and any embarrassment it may have caused our viewers," the station said in a prepared statement.

The photo was of a young woman, identified as Jackson Nurse, who posed in the nude for the current issue of *Playboy*.

The station was putting together an item for the evening news on the photo when a technician pressed the wrong button and the picture popped up on the screen, temporarily interrupting "Another World," officials said.

The station said it was deluged with calls, most objecting to the photo.

A few asked to see it again.

Suit Claims Pizza Led to Dog's Demise

SANDUSKY, OHIO (UPI) A couple who ate a pizza they claimed was spoiled are blaming the pizza maker for the death of the family's pet dog.

Joyce and David White of Berlin Heights are asking an Erie County Common Pleas Court for $125,000 in damages from the Natilina Pizza Co. of Elyria. The Whites said they suffered emotional distress by eating a spoiled pizza, which subsequently led to the death of their pet on April 26, 1986.

The dog, Fluffy, didn't eat the pizza. But when the Whites did, they allegedly became violently ill. Fluffy was killed when the Whites ran over the dog in the driveway while seeking medical assistance, the suit claims.

The Whites ate a small quantity of the "spoiled, rotten, rancid and moldy" pizza, the suit claims. The expiration date on the pizza was April 18 and [it was] labeled edible for human consumption seven days after that date.

The couple claim the pizza maker and the grocery store, Pick and Pay of Sandusky, negligently manufactured and sold the product.

The defendants could not be reached for comment.

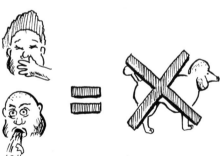

Young Russian Couple Asks for "Protection"

SHANNON, IRELAND (UPI) A young Russian couple caused an embarrassing mix-up at Shannon Airport when they were mistaken for political defectors.

The pair, on a technical stopover on the Havana-Moscow Aeroflot route, approached a counter at the big Shannon duty-free store Monday. In halting English the man asked for "protection," according to an airport spokesman.

He was quickly whisked away for questioning by Immigration authorities. But after 20 minutes officials determined it was not political protection he was after, but sexual protection. He just wanted to buy some condoms.

It was the sort of merchandise the Soviets should have expected they could purchase in the West.

But even after authorities understood what the young lovers wanted, the couple could not be helped. In Roman Catholic Ireland the sale of condoms is forbidden except to married couples, and then only with a doctor's prescription.

Embarrassing Welcome

SAN JOSE, CALIFORNIA (AP) A banner that took three months to finish was supposed to say "welcome" in Tagalog, the chief native language of the Philippines. But its message left some red-faced instead of warm-hearted.

An embarrassed Filipino security guard noticed the mistake in the banner that went up outside the San Jose Public Library on Wednesday. Senior librarian K. Christie Vogel said the guard explained that the $10,000 sign translated to "circumcision."

"There was a heck of a lot of scurrying around... when we found out," she said.

The error was found in the 30-foot-high banner with messages in 27 languages that was on display for the library's rededication. It was renamed after slain civil rights leader Martin Luther King, Jr., whose birthday is observed Monday.

Greetings in other languages also were wrong; "welcome" in Swedish and Dutch both were misspelled.

Vogel said librarians worked with officials from the city's redevelopment office to collect greetings from reference books. The greetings were compiled and sent to a San Francisco sign company that handled the painting.

A four-person crew took the banner down.

Love Is Blind

NEW DELHI, INDIA (AP) Two Hindu brides, their vision obstructed by long veils, married the wrong men—giving new meaning to the expression "love is blind."

The Times of India said today that two marriage parties arrived at the same time Tuesday in Patan village in the central Indian state of Madhya Pradesh.

There could be no exchange of spouses...

The ceremonies were rushed, and the long veils obscured the brides' vision, preventing them from picking out their true fiancés, the report said.

Following Hindu tradition, one bride circled a fire with a bridegroom seven times, sealing the marriage. The other bride then completed "the seven steps" with the second bridegroom, the paper said.

When they lifted their veils, the brides discovered they had married the wrong men.

But village elders said that "the seven perambulations around the sacred fire" were final and there could be no exchange of spouses, the paper said.

Most marriages in rural India are arranged, especially among Hindus, who comprise 82 percent of India's 880 million people.

What If They're Write?

LAND O'LAKES, FLORIDA (UPI) School officials sent out an anti-illiteracy campaign flyer that said, "By the year 2000... let's overcome literacy."

Labored Breeding

LEESVILLE, LOUISIANA (AP) Parents sent the following excuses to school on behalf of their children.

"My son is under doctor's care and should not take P.E. today. Please execute him."

"Please excuse Fred for being. It was his father's fault."

"Please excuse Mary from Jim yesterday. She is administrating."

"Please excuse Fred for being absent. He had a cold and could not breed well."

"Please excuse Mary from being absent yesterday. She was in bed with gramps."

The school official who compiled the list changed all the names to either Fred or Mary, to protect the guilty.

Tom, Dick and Hairy

Hindu Holy Man Performs Bizarre Feat

HARDWAR, INDIA (Reuters) The naked sadhu (holy man) puffed hashish from a clay pipe as he sat outside his tent recounting the ascetic traditions of his ancient Hindu sect.

Mawant Godavari Giri, who said he is 85 and lives half the year alone in a Himalayan cave, spoke of nudity, celibacy, fire-worship and deathlike trances—and of bizarre physical feats beyond the ability of most men.

Under British rule in India, Godavari mentioned casually to the listeners seated outside his tent, a naga (naked holy man) of his Juna Akhara sect pulled a locomotive some distance by his penis.

"Since then we have the unwritten right to travel first class in Indian trains for free," he said with a chuckle.

Questioned by an incredulous Western journalist, he insisted that similar exploits were performed to this day.

Strengthening the male organ to perform prodigious feats, Godavari said, "is part of a training which disciplines the body to survive in any type of condition with the minimum comforts.

"In the later stages of life," he added with a smile, "such a feat becomes a holy man's real credential, so that people do not consider him a fake."

Only last month, here in Hardwar beside the Ganges, a sadhu had pulled two jeeps about 25 feet along a road with his penis. Godavari said. After the foreign reporter persisted in his questions, the lean old holy man stood up, shook his plaited, ground-length hair out of a coiled bun, and announced: "I have sent for a heavy stone."

Amid laughter from his admirers he added: "Here is another representative of the British... so let's impress them again."

Two men brought a large rock in a rickshaw and rolled it up to the tent. The journalist drew guffaws as he failed to lift it with his hands. It must have weighed 220 pounds.

Undaunted, the naked sadhu crouched over the rock, knees bent, and slipped his penis through the loop of pink cloth that his followers tied round the rock.

He gripped his penis with both hands and heaved upwards. For an instant the rock rose a fraction of an inch into the air before thudding back to earth.

"Is that enough, or do you want me to throw it into the heavens," the old man grinned triumphantly.

Thai Worker Cuts Off Penis Because Wife Left Him

BAHRAIN (Reuters) A Thai Construction worker in Bahrain, depressed that his wife had left him, cut off his penis.

Consultant urologist Dr. Mohammed Durazi told Reuters on Monday his friends discovered him bleeding, put his severed penis in a bottle of water and drove it and him to hospital.

Durazi said he took three hours to sew the penis on again last Monday. "The organ is functioning well," he added. "He is much better now, talking and smiling with his friends."

Chinese Surgeons Successfully Lengthen Too-Short Penis

BEIJING (AFP) Two Shanghai surgeons have successfully lengthened the penis of a man who complained that his sexual organ was too short, a Shanghai newspaper reported Friday.

The newspaper, *Wenhui Bao*, said that Huang Wenyi and Cheng Kaixiang, the two chief surgeons at Shanghai People's Hospital No. 9, took flesh and skin from the patient's forearm and grafted it on the tip of the organ.

The hospital has said that it would accept foreign patients.

Man Arranges His Own Death After Baldness Cure Fails

LONDON (Reuters) A man depressed by baldness arranged for a friend to kill him after an operation on his testicles failed to stop his hair loss, a court heard on Monday.

A prosecutor told the court in the southwestern English city of Bristol that Barry Palmer, 50, had "picked up a notion that if he had a surgical operation on his testicles, that would stop his hair falling out."

He said Palmer persuaded a surgeon to carry out the operation a year ago, but did not specify what it involved.

Desperate over the failure of the treatment, Palmer arranged for Brett Cooper, 17, to smother him to death after giving him tablets to make him drowsy, the court heard. Palmer was found dead in his garage.

Cooper denied murder.

Vasectomies for King's Birthday

BANGKOK, THAILAND (UPI) More than 700 men underwent free seven-minute vasectomies to celebrate the King's birthday, Thailand's Population and Community Development Association said.

The Association said 719 men lined up Sunday outside tents festooned with inflated, brightly colored condoms and signs calling for fewer children, in front of the National Lottery Bureau.

The seven-minute sterilization operations were performed free of charge in honor of the 55th birthday of King Bhumibol Adulyadej, the Association said.

The Community Development Association has arranged free vasectomies on May 1 and the King's birthday for several years as part of its successful drive to lower Thailand's birth rate, which has dropped from an average of 3.3 children per family to 1.8 per family in the past 10 years.

"The United Nations has called that the most dramatic drop in population growth in recorded history," Mechai Viravaidya, the Population and Community Development Association's Secretary General, said Sunday.

One man said he was inspired to undergo the 7-minute procedure by a popular song called "I'm Vasectomized," which currently ranks No. 3 in Thailand.

Another man, carrying a month-old baby, said before heading into a tent for his operation, "I had four children and decided to have a vasectomy a year ago, but I waited too long."

Sunday's sterilization program exceeded the record 661 vasectomies performed last May Day, the Association said.

Stupid Human Tricks

Microwaved Hot Dog Lives to Wag Her Tail

TORONTO (Reuters) Kizi, the miniature schnauzer dog, is recovering from being microwaved after an intruder popped her in the oven.

Kizi escaped with a limp and a burnt ear after the metal buckle on her dog collar shorted the oven, her owner said.

"We think he set the timer for nine minutes. She had a metal buckle on her collar and that shorted the oven. That saved her life," said Kizi's owner, 13-year-old Chad Leis, from Kitchener in Ontario, Canada.

A 14-year-old boy has been charged with cruelty.

Canned Kid

PROVIDENCE, R.I. (AP) Getting a 2-year-old out of an old-fashioned 40-quart milk can was more than rescue workers could handle, but a physician solved the puzzle by treating it like a case of childbirth.

Robyn Daigneault's parents kept the 35-inch-high milk can around as a bank for pennies. Robyn apparently had gotten into it before, but had never slipped below the neck of the container as she did Tuesday, said her mother Roberta.

Robyn's 4-year-old brother Roy raised the alarm, "yelling, 'Ma! Robyn's stuck in the penny bank!'" Mrs. Daigneault said Thursday.

Robyn's shoulders became wedged against the sides of the can and even promises of ice cream and lollipops couldn't get her to put her arms up through the milk can's neck so she could be pulled out. She wouldn't budge even when rescue workers promised her a ride on a fire engine.

So the canned tot was taken to Rhode Island Hospital, where Dr. Larry Proano decided against cutting torches or trying to slide her out with gallons of mineral oil.

She wouldn't budge, even when rescue workers promised her a ride on a fire engine.

Proano considered Robyn's position, then upended the milk can while nurse Dennis McKenna positioned himself like an obstetrician.

Out popped Robyn's head.

"Then we delivered the shoulders, one at a time just like a baby," Proano said.

Robyn, whose delivery was accompanied by about 5,000 pennies spilling from the bank, was none the worse for the experience, her mother said.

Prison Trivia

The jail's staff was stumped...

BOSTON (AP) When an inmate at the Deer Island jail climbed up on the facility's roof, he stumped the officials trying to coax him down by making a demand only the most ardent student of mid-1970s television trivia could meet.

The inmate said he wouldn't descend until someone could come up with the names of all six children on the popular television series "The Brady Bunch," said Deputy Penal Commissioner George Romanos.

The jail's staff was stumped, but the inmate, whose name was withheld because no charges were filed in the incident, came down after a standoff of more than five hours.

Romanos said the inmate, who has been jailed since October for receiving a stolen vehicle, wrapped himself in a sheet and used scaffolding to scale the five-floor prison on Tuesday afternoon.

"He did this on a lark," said Romanos, adding that he didn't know whether the inmate would be disciplined.

And, for the sake of appeasing tormented trivia buffs, the names of the television kids were Marcia, Greg, Jan, Peter, Cindy and Bobby.

Tank-Vodka Barter

FRANKFURT, WEST GERMANY (AP) Four Soviet soldiers lost while on maneuvers in Czechoslovakia traded their tank to a tavern owner for two cases of vodka and were found sleeping off the liquor in a forest two days later, a West German newspaper reported.

Communist authorities later learned that the saloon keeper dismantled the tank and sold the pieces to a local metal-recycling center, the *Frankfurter Allgemeine Zeitung* daily reported in its weekend edition.

The incident was reported in an article written by Ota Filip, a Czechoslovak emigré author who contributes periodically to the conservative newspaper.

Reached by telephone Sunday at his home in Munich, Filip said the episode occurred last fall during large Warsaw Pact maneuvers in Czechoslovakia. He said he learned of it in a letter from reliable sources passed on to him three weeks ago.

Filip's story, quoting a report by police in eastern Bohemia province in Czechoslovakia, related the incident as follows:

A four-man Soviet tank crew participating in maneuvers got lost as darkness fell in cold, rainy, foggy weather. Their vodka was running out, since rations had been cut as part of a Soviet government campaign against alcoholism.

Around 8 p.m., the tank crew drove into a village where the only pub was still open. They parked the tank in a barn behind the building and walked into the pub as the proprietor was about to close.

The crew had money for one more bottle of vodka, but bought three more after the crew leader plunked down his gold wedding ring.

At 11:15 p.m., the crew was spotted leaving the pub with two cases of vodka and nearly seven pounds of herring and pickles.

The tankers, found snoozing in a forest two days later, told local authorities and Soviet military police they did not know what happened to the tank.

The first clue turned up 10 days later when the head of a local metal-recycling center said he had just bought a large amount of high-quality, sawed-up steel from a pub owner.

Investigators soon found the shell of the tank in the barn behind the pub. The proprietor told authorities he had acquired the tank for 24 bottles of vodka with herring and pickles thrown in "as a gesture of comradeship."

Filip told The Associated Press the fate of the pub owner and the Soviet soldiers was not known.

Dwarfs

SYDNEY, AUSTRALIA (UPI) A "dwarf-throwing and bowling contest" to be held in major Australian cities next month drew outcries Thursday from dwarfs and government officials—but there's no way they can stop it.

The Australian *People* magazine earlier announced it would stage the charity event between teams from Australia and England in Brisbane, Sydney and Melbourne in November.

Each team would consist of one muscular thrower and one dwarf, a professional stuntman wearing a crash helmet, who would be hurled for distance onto a padded mat.

The contest, first staged in Brisbane last year, will feature "dwarf bowling" as an added event, according to *People* magazine editor David Naylor.

"We're going to strap a skateboard to their stomachs, and roller skates to their arms, and roll them down an expansive floor toward the skittles," Naylor said.

In Melbourne, the secretary of the Little People's Association of Australia in Victoria State, Jennifer Johnson, attacked the event as humiliating and degrading to the dwarf community and called on the government to stop it.

"I think it's disgusting—it's an appalling idea," Johnson said. "And I talk for the hundreds of people within my association, and we are totally against it."

A spokesman for the New South Wales police minister, George Paciullo, conceded that dwarf-throwing is in bad taste, but there is no law against it.

Naylor, who said proceeds from the "test match" series would go to charity, said the event does not humiliate dwarfs.

"The two dwarfs we are using are not representing other dwarfs," he said. "They are professional stuntmen who like being thrown. They are professional projectiles."

Tavern Times Fast Dog Food Feasts

EUGENE, ORE. (AP) A tavern is offering $500 to whomever eats a can of dog food the fastest—and it can't be a dog.

"It sells a lot of beer," said Bill Rogers, manager of The Cooler tavern where the dog-food-eating contest is being held for bar patrons.

Every other Saturday since mid-October, contestants have lined up to eat a can of dog food in hopes of competing in the Great Dog Food Eat-Off Jan. 29.

The winner will get $500, and $300 will be distributed among the other seven finalists.

"It's gross, but you do it," said Paul Sheriff, a former University of Oregon wrestler who won the latest gobbling event Saturday in 1 minute 59 seconds as onlookers cheered.

Rogers holds the tavern's record, consuming one bowl in 1 minute and 14 seconds.

A one-pound can of the wet, slimy beef-and-soybean dog food is emptied into each bowl on a plywood-covered pool table.

The food retains the can's cylindrical shape until the contestants, hands

"It's gross, but you do it."

behind backs, plunge their faces into the bowl while a stopwatch is used to time them.

"When you're done,"emcee David Clyde told the contestants Saturday night, "simply raise your head and respond with 'Arf, arf.'"

Rogers said 23 people participated in the preliminaries, and 19 others paid $10 entry fees but failed to show up.

"There won't be any women in the finals," Rogers said. "Two women did it, but neither could finish a can and they didn't want to try it again."

Dave Chesney, a supervisory investigator with the U.S. Food and Drug Administration in Portland, said there are no additives used in the dog food that are different from those used in human food.

"I thought it was going to come back up there at the end," said Jim Clingman, the only contestant Saturday to have practiced eating dog food at home. "This is definitely the last time I'm going to do it."

Prisoner Claims Slaying Saved Money

CHICAGO (UPI) A Federal appeals court has turned down a federal prisoner's contention he saved the government money by killing a fellow inmate in 1983.

A three-judge panel of the 7th U.S. Circuit Court of Appeals on Wednesday upheld a lower court order requiring inmate George House to pay the government $1,303.61 for autopsy, funeral and burial expenses of Jack Callison, who was killed in 1983 at the federal prison in Marion.

House pleaded guilty to voluntary manslaughter and another 10 years was added to his sentence in addition to the restitution order. House, 34, of Greenville, Miss., is serving 25 years for armed robbery and is supposed to be released from Marion in 1989.

He contended he saved the government money by stabbing Callison, who was serving 25 years for bank robbery.

The Marion prison charges the state $76.03 a day for housing a prisoner.

> **"The policy of the United States was that Callison should live."**

"Although chutzpah sometimes pays off, House cannot escape so easily," Judge Frank Easterbrook wrote in the eight-page opinion.

"This [case] does not depend on net loss.... The policy of the United States was that Callison should live," he wrote.

The judges also rejected House's argument that his poverty made restitution inappropriate and that the Bureau of Prisons had unfairly frozen his commissary account, depriving him of candy, potato chips, running shoes and other personal items.

"One may doubt whether deprivation of potato chips is an appropriate maximum punishment for manslaughter, but it was the only one available to the sentencing court," the judge wrote. "House wants his chocolate and cannot get it."

Ants Scrub Wedding

NAIROBI, KENYA (UPI) An unfortunate farmer had to call off his wedding because an army of ants ate $150 worth of banknotes he buried for safety in his garden.

He couldn't pay the dowry, the Kenya News Agency said Wednesday.

The ants ate 2,000 shillings ($150) in cash, which represented the life savings of the farmer from Isiolo in northern Kenya, the agency said.

The report said the farmer gathered what was left of the banknotes and took them to the district officer in Isiolo, 400 miles north of Nairobi.

Officer Laban Ohito said he could not refund the money.

He warned farmers to keep their money in a bank rather than buried in the ground as is the custom in rural Kenya.

Out of embarrassment, the farmer requested anonymity.

Another Japanese Quake? No, Just a Rock Concert

TOKYO (Reuters) Officials investigating mysterious tremors that have been shaking houses in part of a Japanese city have found the cause—not an earthquake, but rock fans jumping up and down at a local nightclub.

The environment office in Kawasaki, south of Tokyo, Tuesday ordered the Club Citta to thicken its floors with concrete. At the club, which has no seats, up to 1,100 fans have been jumping up and down in unison at nightly concerts.

Tremors in places near the club registered up to five on the Japanese intensity scale of seven, enough to damage houses and cause furniture to fall.

Lightning Strikes Lawyer Dead

SHREVEPORT, LA (UPI) Maverick lawyer N. Graves Thomas stood in a boat during a thunderstorm, raised his hands and proclaimed heavenward, "Here I am." Moments later a lightning bolt struck him dead, witnesses said.

The lightning bolt struck Thomas in the head Monday aboard his new ski boat on Lake Bistineau. Death apparently was instantaneous as there was no exit point for the lightning, Bossier Parish sheriff's spokesman Scott Hodges said.

Three people were in the boat with Thomas and a young woman was in the water preparing to ski, despite heavy storms that had rumbled through much of the state, officials said.

Witnesses said Thomas, 40, stood in the back of the boat, raised his hands toward the sky and said, "Here I am." Quickly, the lightning bolt struck his head.

Dr. Denny Gamble, who was on a houseboat nearby, tried unsuccessfully to revive Thomas, who was pronounced dead at Riverside Medical Center in Bossier City.

A former state prosecutor and assistant U.S. attorney, Thomas was at the time of his death representing Ronald Richie of Lake Bistineau, who was accused of recklessness in a boating accident this month that killed three people on the lake.

Attorneys who worked with or against Thomas, whose family includes several judges and lawyers, described him as a firebrand and a maverick but a strong advocate for his often notorious clients—including police killers, reputed crime figures, accused white collar criminals and drug smugglers.

Metal in Bra Attracted Fatal Bolt

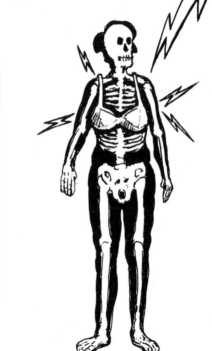

LONDON (UPI) Iris Sommerville's bra killed her, a coroner ruled yesterday. Dr. Paul Knapman held that a metal-reinforced bra worn by the 62-year-old woman as she strolled through a park in a storm this month attracted a deadly lightning bolt. "It is one of those cases, if ever there was one, which is an example of an act of God," Knapman said.

Pathologist Iain West testified at the inquest that a burn mark on Sommerville's chest appeared to match exactly the reinforced metal area of the bra, and he agreed the metal apparently attracted the bolt.

It Came in Through the Bathroom Window

It Came in Through the Bathroom Window

BURLINGTON, VT. (UPI) A man sitting on the toilet reading the newspaper was interrupted Friday by a dump truck that crashed into his house, overturned and spilled sand over him and his bathroom floor.

"It missed me by 7 or 8 feet," said Edward Brisson, who was not injured. "A little closer and he would have had me. It was strange."

Police said truckdriver Lawrence Pecor, 64, of Essex, apparently lost his brakes as he approached an intersection. The truck, carrying 14 tons of sand, careened around the corner, jumped a curve and slammed into Brisson's home.

The cab hit the house sideways, rolling over and destroying much of a front room in the house. As it rolled, the truck threw sand through the window of a bathroom adjacent to the front room, said Brisson's son, John.

"My dad was sitting on the toilet reading the paper and they filled him with sand," said the son.

The elder Brisson said the sand pouring through the bathroom window "got all over me."

The truck caught fire, but it was quickly extinguished by firemen.

Pecor got a bump on his head, but was not hospitalized.

Erupting Toilet

WILLIAMSPORT, MD. (AP) Donald and Nancy Barnhart's bathroom has an unusual feature—an erupting toilet.

Over the last three years, the commode in their home has been known to make a burping sound before shooting a blast of water to the ceiling.

"It's rather exciting, and embarrassing," said Barnhart of the toilet's occasional lapse of manners. So far, it hasn't unleashed a geyser when a visitor was using the bathroom, he said.

The Barnharts said the problem began when the town installed a pump on its sewage system to cope with development in the area.

Town officials blame the spouting toilet on an underground "ejector" which is supposed to force sewage uphill with air pressure. If the air compressor fails to shut off, the pressure is released through a nearby manhole—and the Barnharts' toilet.

Town Manager M. Lee Draper said officials believe the problem stems from an electronic probe that activates the pump. He said there was no estimate of when the problem might be corrected.

Singapore's "Loo Patrol" Catches Non-Flushers

SINGAPORE, (Reuters) Singapore's "Loo Patrol," on the lookout for public toilet users who fail to flush, have nabbed the first offenders under a new flushing law.

Health inspectors have booked 17 people so far under the law, which came into force on July 1st, making it an offense not to flush after using a public toilet, an Environment Ministry spokesman said on Tuesday.

Offenders are liable to a fine of up to 1,000 Singapore dollars (500 U.S.) each time they forget to pull the flush chain. However, the 17 were let off with a warning during a two-week grace period, he said.

Health inspectors are required to check public toilets for offenders and cleanliness during their inspections of public buildings, he said.

Wild Kingdom

Bird Makes Monkeys of Would-be Captors

HEALDSBURG, CALIF. (UPI) An escaped macaw parrot has turned sarcastic as well as elusive, screeching taunts such as "Hello, dodo" to her frustrated would-be captors.

Remington, a 9-year-old female, has been soaring among the 100-foot-high treetops in town, living on walnuts, figs and grapes since escaping from her owner Oct. 10.

Among those trying to catch her have been firefighters, a tree surgeon, neighbors, city public-works employees and animal control officers.

"We've been chasing that bird all over town and we can't even get close to getting it," firefighter Charlie Jurecek said.

Even when they have been able to approach the bird, it hasn't done any good.

"She's getting real sarcastic," her owner, Patricia Foss, said. "Not long after she got away...I was within inches of her when she yelled out, 'Hello, dodo,' and took off."

"She's getting real sarcastic."

"Then, from the next tree, she screeched, "I can talk. Can you fly?"

Foss said the parrot, which had never before escaped, flew off after she had bathed her and put her out to dry.

Workers were trying to think of new schemes to catch her, including possibly using a tranquilizer shot from a blow gun or trapping her with another macaw.

Oscar the Lobster Saved from Kettle

TACOMA, WASH. (UPI) Suzanne Brown cradled Oscar in her hands, ready to boil him alive to please her husband, but one pleading look from his beady little eyes and she was spending the night cozily hand-feeding him.

"I kind of fell in love with a lobster. I even pet him. When I talk to him his eyes roll back," Brown said Wednesday, more than a week after she began hand-feeding the crustacean on Valentine's Day.

Brown's husband is being surprisingly supportive, but her friends think she's a little off.

But the union was not to last, because it wasn't long before Brown learned that Oscar is a she, who would have to return home to the East Coast in order to survive. She said the lobster will be flown to Massachusetts to take a dive off a pier and swim for his life.

The company that caught Oscar has agreed to give the critter another chance by throwing him off a pier at Gloucester, Massachusetts, where he was caught.

Suzanne bought Oscar for $14 from

"When I talk to him his eyes roll back."

a seafood store, but when it came time to do the dirty deed, the boiling water just looked too cruel.

"I decided I wanted to keep him for a pet. I only wanted to save a lobster's life," Brown said.

Howard Frisk, a sales manager for International Lobster of Gloucester, said the request to return Oscar to her home is an unusual one, but he'll do it, though there's no guarantee she'll be any happier.

"He (she) could live for another 50 years, or he (she) could get caught next week," Frisk said.

Attorneys Smell a Rat in Public Defender's Office

LAGUNA NIGUEL, CALIFORNIA (AP) As any prosecutor can tell you, there are rats and snakes in the public defender's office.

A plan to exterminate the rodents, rabbits and reptiles that burrow inside the trailer-office from a nearby field has backfired, with the animals dying in the walls and floorboards and the lawyers scurrying away.

"The place had become very malodorous," said Carl Holmes, chief deputy public defender. "It stunk."

Unable to work any longer, the lawyers, investigators and secretaries sought temporary office space in the South Orange County Municipal courthouse, a situation that created some problems with attorney-client privacy.

The county is paying $4,000 a day to hire outside attorneys to handle misdemeanor cases because the public defenders have no place to speak with clients privately.

Municipal Court Judge Pamela Iles said she doesn't blame the public defenders.

"The place had become very malodorous."

"When we were pulling a dead rat a week out of the Public Defender's Office it got to be too much," Ms. Iles said.

County officials agreed the trailer is uninhabitable and said they're working to find new office space as soon as possible.

Cats Go Wacky Over Wax

WASHINGTON (UPI) A scientist is looking for answers about why his normally finicky cats have a strange appetite for human earwax.

In a letter published in the British scientific journal *Nature*, Thomas Arny, a physicist at the University of Massachusetts, seeks suggestions from the research community on why his two Siamese cats are so fond of the substance.

The cats' craving for earwax is so great, Arny said, that one "leaps on the bed in the morning hoping to be offered some."

When the Massachusetts scientist mentioned his pets' odd behavior to three other people, he said they told him their cats also had a fondness for wax.

"I'd always thought that earwax tasted very bitter (as a deterrent to

insects getting into your ears), so I find the cats' reaction hard to understand," Arny wrote.

"Do any of your readers have any explanation? I wonder if it might be a means to induce cats to groom their kittens," he asked.

Arny could not be reached Wednesday to comment further on details of his unusual research project.

U.S. veterinary experts, none of whom wished to be named, said they had never heard of felines going crazy over earwax, although some pointed out that cats often like to play with cotton or the cotton swabs many people use to clean their ears.

75

Two Pitbulls Downed by Police Bullets

MANNINGTON, WEST VIRGINIA (UPI) Two large pitbulls trying to devour a 600-pound cow alive were downed by police bullets as they rushed to attack two officers, collapsing dead just short of their targets.

Police Chief David James and another officer shot and killed the two animals after finding them eating a live cow.

"They just looked at us and let go of the cow and came for us," James said Thursday. "I guess they thought we were going to take it away from them."

James estimated the larger dog at about 90 pounds and the smaller in the 60–70 pound range. When found Tuesday, the two dogs had wrestled a 600-pound cow to the ground, dragged it about 125 yards under a corncrib and were eating it alive.

"It was just unbelievable," said James. "They were actually eating it alive."

James, thinking that "most dogs will run," first tried to stomp his feet

"It could have been like the Little Big Horn."

and shout at the pitbulls, but that only encouraged them to rush him and Patrolman Donald Wheeler.

The chief fired two .357 Magnum bullets at the biggest one, but the animal continued to charge. Wheeler put three more bullets in the larger dog before it collapsed less than 10 feet from him. James shot the smaller dog three times before it died within 10 feet of him.

James said his first thought when he saw the dogs racing toward him was, "Well, (expletive)."

The chief said he did not realize he had only one bullet remaining after shooting the smaller dog, saying he was trying to remember where the nearest tree was.

The dog's owners will have to make restitution to Don Snider, owner of the cow, which was valued at $600, said James.

He said the dogs' owners "seem to believe we shouldn't have had any right to shoot their dogs." James added that he was glad there were not more pitbulls because "it could have been like the Little Big Horn."

Wild Elephants Kill Sleeping Couple

KATMANDU, NEPAL (AP) Seven wild elephants wandered into a village, drank a large jug of home-brewed liquor and went on a rampage, killing a couple as they slept, a news agency reported Thursday.

Chakra Bahadur Rai and his wife were killed by the elephants Wednesday in Barachhetra village of Sunsari district, 100 miles east of Katmandu, the Nepalese news agency RSS reported.

The elephants also destroyed houses and grain in storage before villagers chased them away with torches, RSS added. The elephants then entered a nearby village and destroyed crops, a bridge and more houses, the news agency said.

$16 Million Jet Destroyed after Colliding with Pigs on Runway

JACKSONVILLE, FLA. (AP) A pair of wild pigs that wandered off course got hit by an F-18 fighter, forcing the pilot to eject as the jet veered off a runway and crashed at Jacksonville International Airport.

The pigs were killed. The pilot was bruised. The $16 million jet was destroyed.

The pilot, Lt. Col. Sam Carter, said Wednesday that he has heard his fill of oinker jokes, including his wife's offer to let him pig out on a pork dinner.

Berserk Blackbird Buzzing the Boulevard

SANTA MONICA, CALIF. (AP) A berserk blackbird has been buzzing Wilshire Boulevard, divebombing at people's heads, pecking and kicking them with its claws, say those who work in the area.

"Favorite targets seem to be bald men," said Sue Foster, a Red Cross worker who witnessed some of the attacks.

"Funniest thing I've ever seen," said C. J. Hafner, manager at Bob Burns restaurant. "He dives down and sort of kicks people with his claws."

The bird's antics around 2nd Street and Wilshire have provided entertainment for those with roofs over their heads.

"I went into one building down there, and everyone was at the window watching the bird dive at people," Ms. Foster said.

Stan Hernacki of Santa Monica Animal Control said his office "got a complaint of a bird swooping down and pecking people."

Favorite targets seem to be bald men.

Kimbail Garrett, an ornithologist at the Los Angeles County Museum of Natural History, offered an explanation Monday.

"This is nesting time, and its eggs have probably just hatched," Garrett said. "They can be very aggressive and protective when they see anything they perceive as a predator. But this [swooping] probably will go on for only a few more weeks," until the chicks have grown.

Beer-Drinking Burro Retires on Short Rations

HAVANA, CUBA (Reuters) Pancho, a 30-year-old burro who drinks 30 liters of beer a day, has been ordered to cut down his drinking by veterinarians who say he has a liver problem.

The veterinarians say Pancho, who is nationally known, must stop entertaining customers by drinking beer in a bar overlooking the Mayabe Valley in eastern Cuba, the Havana-based news agency Prensa Latina reported on Saturday.

Pancho must be put out to pasture, but is not going on the wagon, the agency said. Aware that withdrawal might be bad for Pancho, veterinarians allowed him 10 liters a day.

Pancho began boozing 15 years ago when a patron gave him a bottle of beer and he delighted customers by braying for more. Patrons have been standing him drinks ever since.

Seeing Eye Dog Sees Too Much in Delivery Room

SURREY, BRITISH COLUMBIA (AP) A guide dog accompanied a blind couple into a hospital delivery room but got sick twice during the woman's labor and had to leave the room.

But Rick Oakes and his wife, Chantal, said they wouldn't have wanted their dog to miss the birth of their daughter, Whitney Leanne Oakes.

"I like that dog better than some people I know," Mrs. Oakes said Monday at their home in this Vancouver suburb. "He's just like part of the family."

Oakes said the presence of Bryor, a 3-year-old golden retriever, allowed him to leave for meals and an occasional cigarette during the 24 hours his wife was in labor at Vancouver's Grace Hospital on March 8.

He said he also wanted to make a point after having had his right to have Bryor with him challenged by

> **They wouldn't have wanted their dog to miss the birth of their daughter...**

everyone from taxi drivers to restaurant owners.

"I thought it would be a golden opportunity to let people know guide dogs can go anywhere," he said.

Except for two times when he had to leave the delivery room to throw up, Bryor didn't create problems. When attention focused on the baby after delivery, however, the dog picked up a towel and started dragging it around the room to attract attention to himself.

That's understandable, since everyone from doctors to orderlies had been dropping by to give him a scratch under the collar, Mrs. Oakes said.

Her obstetrician, Barry Sanders, had no qualms about the dog.

"It was an unusual request," he said, "but the dog is great. He would never bother anybody."

It Was Apparently a Very Large Duck

CAMBRIDGE, MD. (UPI) A medical helicopter carrying an amputation patient was forced into an emergency landing when a duck shattered its windshield, smacked the pilot's forehead and ricocheted around the cabin, authorities said Sunday.

"It came right through the glass and struck the pilot in the forehead," State Police spokesman Dan McCarthy said of the Saturday night incident. "It was apparently a very large duck."

Man Bites Dog

Man Complains of Cold, Bites Off Colleague's Ear

DUBAI, UNITED ARAB EMIRATES (Reuters) Pakistani tailor Mohammed Ghulam was too cold and his colleague refused to turn off the air conditioner. So he bit off his ear.

Ghulam, 48, was sentenced to three years in jail for assault, but following an impassioned plea by the victim, the judge reduced the term to three months.

Man Bites Several Passengers Aboard Varig Flight

RIO DE JANEIRO (AFP) A 26-year-old Uruguayan man bit several of his 179 fellow passengers aboard a Varig jetliner Monday, on a flight from Costa Rica to Rio de Janeiro, police said.

Overpowered by crew members, Adolfo Umpierrez was bound and gagged, turned over to police on landing, and was being prepared for return to Uruguay on the next available flight, airline sources said.

They said Mr. Umpierrez's teeth were filed down to sharp points.

No reason was immediately given for the man's behavior.

Breakfast had just been served, one crew member noted, so the man could not have been hungry.

A Do-It-Yourselfer

NANCY, FRANCE (Reuters) A young Frenchwoman who tried to bite a policeman after her Alsatian dog refused to do so was sentenced today to a three-month suspended sentence and a $450 fine.

Policeman's Painful Arrest

HARARE, ZIMBABWE (AFP) A woman arrested by a policeman in Zimbabwe for selling fruit without a permit retaliated by biting off a large portion of flesh from his private parts," the state news agency ZIANA reported Thursday.

It said the policeman was receiving medical treatment "and is having difficulty in walking."

Lost Pinkie Wins Woman $55,000

SALINAS, CALIF. (UPI) An acupuncturist who alleged that her ex-husband's dinner date bit off her right pinkie has been awarded $55,000 by a Superior Court jury.

Wah-Ja Kim, 58, said she could not effectively stick pins in her patients' bodies without her pinkie.

Kim said the loss posed a serious religious problem, saying the Confucianism of her native Korea demands "that every human being should have a perfect, whole body to join our ancestors and carry on in the next life."

Kim sued for $1 million, but her lawyer lowered the stakes to $250,000 at the end of the three-day trial, which

Judge Robert O'Farrell described as "something straight out of 'Divorce Court.'"

The jury awarded Kim $55,000 Thursday, with payment split equally between Kim's ex-husband, William W. Hall, 55, and his friend, Jeannie Westall, 45, both of Monterey.

Kim said Westall bit off the fifth finger of her right hand during an altercation on December 19, 1983, at Hall's Monterey condominium. The couple had been separated for about a year. Kim and Hall were divorced later that month.

Taxi Driver Bites Traffic Cop

JOHANNESBURG (AFP) An enraged taxi driver, incensed that his vehicle was about to be towed away, bit a traffic policeman so badly "it looked as if a lion had mauled him," a traffic department spokesman said.

Marius LeGrange, 20, ordered a tow truck to remove a minibus taxi blocking a city center junction, but was attacked by the driver, who ripped the winch off the truck in an effort to drive the taxi away while it was still hooked up.

The taxi driver escaped after the incident Tuesday, but police impounded his vehicle. Mr. LeGrange was taken to hospital.

Finger Lickin' Good

Semen

OMAHA, NEB. (UPI) Whoever swiped two thermos bottles from Charlie Kyser's pickup truck this week probably got a surprise when they opened the bottles.

Kyser told police the stainless steel thermoses were filled with $3,275 worth of bull semen he bought in Omaha for use in his cattle breeding business at Ainsworth, Neb.

Kyser checked into a motel Monday night and left the bottles in the back of the truck, said Police Sgt. Phil Busch.

Sometime between 2 a.m. and 7 a.m. Tuesday someone took the thermoses, one containing semen valued at $3,000 and the other with $275 worth of semen, said Busch.

Mouse

An unexpected ingredient

NEW BRUNSWICK, N.J. (UPI) A man's bowl of Yankee bean soup had an unexpected ingredient—a 4-inch-long mouse—a suit filed in superior court has charged.

Jeffrey Odom, 26, filed suit Tuesday in Middlesex County against the Friendly Ice Cream Restaurant in Woodbridge, seeking unspecified damages.

The suit says Odom was eating the soup last Oct. 18 when he bit into the mouse and consumed part of its tail. He said he was hospitalized for two days and forced to seek psychiatric treatment.

Odom's lawyer, Ronald Brown, said that following the incident a township health inspector ordered an autopsy on the mouse to determine whether it had been placed in the soup after cooking.

Brown said Dr. Edward Greenstein, chief veterinarian at Rutgers University, concluded the mouse had not been boiled or cooked in the soup.

Odom's other lawyer, Andrew Ingram, said his client had not placed the mouse in the soup and that subsequent inspections found "severe (rodent) infestation problems."

The restaurant manager declined comment.

Snake

HAMPTON, IOWA (UPI) A couple has filed suit against the Del Monte Food Company, saying their daughter found a snake's head in a can of green beans.

"If we got the head, we wonder where the rest of the snake is," Sheldon Pratt of Chapin said Wednesday.

Pratt and his wife, Virginia, said they and their daughter, Candi, were "shocked" at the discovery last January. The suit was filed last month in Small Claims Court in Franklin County.

Sheldon said he told his grocer immediately after discovering the head and the grocer pulled all the Del Monte canned vegetable goods from the shelf. The California-based company replaced the cans of food.

Sheldon said Del Monte offered the family $100 to settle but he declined.

His Sentence No Laughing Matter

DENVER (AP) The Colorado Court of Appeals upheld on Thursday the conviction of Filbert G. Maestas, who claimed his constitutional rights were violated when police laughed at him for stealing from a meat processing plant the rectums of 1,200 butchered animals.

Maestas and a companion had been arrested outside a meat warehouse by two officers who found several boxes of meat in their car.

The officers summoned the warehouse manager and he confirmed the rectums, known in the trade as rennets, had been processed by his firm.

Maestas and his companion were being driven to jail, when one of the arresting officers began laughing. He asked the policeman what was so amusing and the officer told him that the beef rennets are inedible rectal tissue usable only in curing cheese.

In plainer language, the officer told Maestas what he had stolen.

Maestas replied. "If I go to jail for stealing 1,200 ——— (rennets), I'm really going to be mad."

...the officer had reason to laugh.

That statement was used against him in his trial. Maestas appealed that the remark was obtained illegally and he was thrown off guard because the officer was laughing.

The court disregarded that argument, saying the officer had reason to laugh.

Felon Food

LANSING, MICHIGAN (AP) Unruly inmates who hurl their food at guards in Michigan prisons will be served entire meals all neatly baked into loaves for less mess, a Department of Corrections spokeswoman said today.

"Instead of giving them a tray full of food, you give them a loaf," spokeswoman Gail Light said. "Three meals a day you get this great big loaf of all your food."

The State Corrections Commission last week passed a policy directive to begin using the loaves, borrowing the idea from other states, Ms. Light said. Instead of serving an unruly prisoner fish, salad, gelatin or other single food items, all of it would be ground up and mixed with pancake batter, then baked.

"We've had a problem over the years (with inmates) throwing food and human waste and other materials at corrections officers," she said. "We found out some other states were using this type of feeding arrangements for people like that."

Inmates who throw their food will be served the loaves until their behavior is curbed, she said. Loaves are easier to clean up, she said.

The biggest food-throwing problem is at the state prison at Marquette, she said. "It's just a tougher group of prisoners. They're not well-behaved," Ms. Light said.

"It's not supposed to be used as punishment," she said of the loaves. "We're seasoning it. I've tasted some of the samples. I wouldn't say it's horrifying. It's all right."

Woman Stung by Scorpion in Popcorn

SANDY, UTAH (AP) A woman eating popcorn out of a bowl she had set down in her garage was stung in the mouth by a scorpion, authorities say.

Diane Bleckert, 56, was treated at Alta View Hospital and released Tuesday, a nursing supervisor said.

The scorpion, a species common to northern Utah that measures about an inch, apparently crawled into the bowl, firefighter Val Farnsworth said.

Blackert was stung on the inside of her lower lip before she bit the scorpion in half, said a hospital spokeswoman who would not give her name.

Pizza Hold-up

BIRMINGHAM, ALA (UPI) Police Friday were looking for a very large woman who robbed a delivery girl of a $17 pizza with everything on it but anchovies.

The woman, described as being "almost 200 pounds," jumped from the bushes Thursday morning in South Birmingham and accosted Brenda Hollingworth, a delivery girl for the Little Italy Pizza Parlor.

Miss Hollingworth was carrying a pizza back to her car because no one answered the door at the apartment number she had been given.

The woman asked Miss Hollingworth if that was the $17 deluxe pizza she had ordered.

"She had to have been the one who called it in because I never told her how much the pizza cost. It was a large pizza with everything on it but anchovies," said Miss Hollingworth.

Miss Hollingworth said the woman told her to wait while she went upstairs for some money, but instead she returned with a revolver. She told the girl she was sorry for the holdup but she "just wanted the pizza."

Miss Hollingworth said the woman "casually walked away with her gun in one hand and the pizza in the other."

Deadly Doritos?

SAN DIEGO (Reuters) Tortilla corn chips can be sharp enough to rip a hole in the esophagus if improperly chewed, a San Diego doctor says.

In a letter to the *New England Journal of Medicine* published earlier this month, George Longstreth said he treated a woman who developed a 5½-inch-long cut down her throat after she swallowed an improperly chewed chip. Minutes later, the 63-year-old woman vomited blood and subsequently developed chest pain.

When doctors peered down her esophagus—the tube leading to the stomach—they discovered a long scar of clotted blood. More clotted blood was found in her stomach.

The woman spent six days in the hospital and experienced pain for two weeks when she swallowed.

Longstreth said when he tested a broken tortilla chip on an esophagus removed during an autopsy, the chip easily cut flesh.

"A poorly chewed tortilla chip," he concluded, "can produce serious injury."

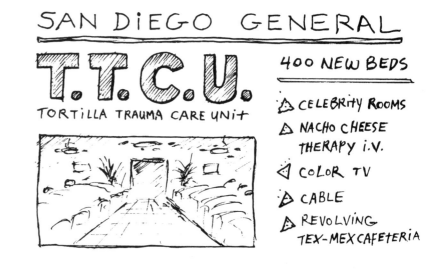

SAN DIEGO GENERAL
T.T.C.U.
TORTILLA TRAUMA CARE UNIT

400 NEW BEDS
- CELEBRITY ROOMS
- NACHO CHEESE THERAPY I.V.
- COLOR TV
- CABLE
- REVOLVING TEX-MEX CAFETERIA

Fifty Ways to Leave Your Lover

Man Gets Divorce From Wife Who Nagged for 34 Years

LONDON (AP) After 34 years of marriage, security officer Percy Adams was granted a divorce Thursday when a High Court judge ruled his wife's nagging was more than he reasonably could be expected to bear.

Chances of reconciliation were "nil."

Gwendoline Adams' careful record-keeping of family grocery purchases and gripes about her husband's snacking caused Adams "a particular amount of bother" and contributed to his high blood pressure, Judge Elizabeth Appleby said.

His wife's comments about his family and his use of their car—which she owned but couldn't drive—were of the sort expected in marriage, but were excessive in Mrs. Adams' case, the judge said.

Adams, 57, left the couple's Chessington home in December 1981 and moved in with another woman a year later.

Mrs. Adams, 55, claimed she still loved him and wanted him back.

The judge said chances of reconciliation were "nil."

Woman's Headache Caused by Bullet in Head

PARIS (Reuters) A 20-year-old French housewife has discovered that a violent headache she suffered for 10 days was caused by a .22 caliber bullet fired at her by her husband while she was asleep.

Evelyne Nuxart, from Saint-Etienne near Lyons, woke up in the middle of the night, last month, and found a trace of blood in her hair. She got up, washed her hair and went back to bed with her husband.

Next day she developed a violent, persistent headache and 10 days later went into hospital. X-rays showed an object in her skull and surgeons extracted a .22 caliber bullet.

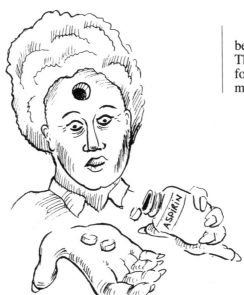

Police said today the husband has been charged with attempted murder. They said he had been out of work for a long time, and decided to commit suicide after killing his wife.

Cheated Husband Exacts Sticky Revenge

SAO PAULO, BRAZIL (AFP) A cuckolded husband, brandishing a revolver and using extra-strong glue for his revenge, cemented his wife's hand to her lover's penis, killing the man, a local newspaper reported Thursday.

The lovers underwent delicate surgery to separate them, but the interloper died several days later from toxic chemicals absorbed through the porous membranes of his penis, the paper said.

Brazilian police declined comment, but legal sources said the husband may face homicide charges.

Illicit Lovers Made Inseparable by Witch Doctors

NAIROBI (Reuter) Two Kenyan lovers had to be taken to hospital this week to be prised apart after the woman's cuckolded husband hired a witch doctor to punish her infidelity, the official Kenya News Agency reported today.

It said the adulterous couple were glued together by a witch doctor's spell during an illicit rendezvous on Wednesday night.

According to the Agency, neighbors who heard the couple's screams called police after trying in vain to pull them apart.

"They were still clinging together," it quoted an eyewitness at the hospital as saying.

Blood and Money—and Bingo

VIROQUA, WIS. (UPI) A 41-year-old woman, convicted of fatally stabbing her husband in order to use his insurance money to pay her bingo debts, was sentenced to life in prison.

A Vernon County jury took five hours Wednesday to convict Carol Alexander of Richland Center, and the judge immediately sentenced her.

Mrs. Alexander was addicted to bingo, prosecutors said during her trial. She collected $65,000 from her husband's insurance and used it to pay her bingo debts.

Mrs. Alexander was charged with first-degree murder in the bedroom stabbing of Donald Alexander, 37, on June 26, 1980. Mrs. Alexander originally told authorities her husband was stabbed in a robbery by two intruders.

Easy Rider

Driving Under the Influence— of a Heater?

INDIANAPOLIS (UPI) A truck driver stopped for drunken driving hadn't been drinking after all, state police said. He was just breathing.

Phillip E. Swanson, a driver from Shamrock Co., was stopped early Thursday on a downtown interstate by Trooper Frank Simmons, who said Swanson's truck was weaving.

The trooper arrested Swanson for drunken driving, then took him to a nearby hospital for a breathalyzer test. Swanson claimed he had not been drinking, and technicians said the test results did not make sense.

Police went back to Swanson's truck and double-checked. They discovered the truck was equipped with an alcohol-fueled heater in the cab.

Swanson apparently accidentally became intoxicated while inhaling the heater fumes, police said. They dropped the charges and put Swanson into a motel room for needed rest.

Suspect Indeed Pickled, Jury Rules

SPOKANE, WASHINGTON (UPI) Zbigniew Krawiec swore that he had just been drinking pickle juice when he was pulled over for drunk driving, but a jury decided he was pickled and convicted him anyway.

Krawiec, a Polish immigrant, said his favorite beverage is pickle juice. It's a Polish custom, he told jurors Thursday.

To prove his point, defense attorney Jim Kane introduced a jar of dill pickles and wanted Krawiec to take a mouthful on the witness stand to prove he loves the stuff.

But deputy prosecutor Steven Nash objected, and Judge Charles Dorn upheld the objection.

"Have I ever seen a 'pickle juice defense' before this? No," said Dorn, who has tried hundreds of drunk-driving cases.

Washington State Trooper Dan Derrick testified that he pulled Krawiec over after spotting him driving with his lights off. Derrick said Krawiec failed a field sobriety test and refused to take a breath test.

Derrick and two jailers testified that the defendant's breath smelled of alcohol, not pickles.

Dorn fined Krawiec $400 and ordered him to serve three days in jail. Kane is expected to appeal.

Turnip was Murder Weapon, Police Say

LONDON (AP) Police say that a 56-year-old man was fatally injured by a turnip hurled from a passing car, and that there have been nearly two dozen other instances of assault with fruits and vegetables.

At an inquest on Monday, Detective Superintendent Graham Howard said the death of Leslie Merry in July was being investigated as a murder.

Merry was hit by a turnip while he was shopping in east London on July 14. He suffered a punctured lung and a rib was broken in three places. His condition worsened after he was released from the hospital on July 16. He was readmitted the next day and died on July 23.

Dr. David Rouse, a pathologist, testified that Merry died of a ruptured spleen, caused by the impact of the turnip, and of acute respiratory failure and chronic pulmonary disease.

Price said a healthier man might have survived the blow.

Howard said there have been a number of incidents in east London in which various fruits and vegetables had been tossed from speeding vehicles. On April 19, he said, a jogger had been hit by a cabbage.

"In many cases where there is no injury the case does not get reported," he said. "Some of the incidents are undoubtedly associated with each other and with the unfortunate killing of Mr. Merry and the injury to a jogger."

Howard said the [jogger's] injuries had included a ruptured stomach and head and facial injuries.

The coroner, Dr. Harold Price, recorded an open verdict, and the investigation continues.

Woman Told Horse Needs Tail Light

KINGMAN, ARIZ. (UPI) A Kingman woman has been ticketed for failure to have a tail light on her horse.

The citation was issued to Kathie T. Smith, 34, after the horse was struck from behind by a car on Hualapai Mountain Road near Kingman about 9 p.m. Tuesday.

Mohave County Sheriff's spokesman Evan Williams said horses are considered "vehicles" and must be equipped for nighttime riding with lights that allow drivers to see them.

Ms. Smith was treated for an injured hip after the accident.

The horse died.

Fred Weyermiller, driver of the car, was not injured.

Oops, Sorry, It's Me Again

RIO DE JANEIRO (Reuters) A driver who lost control of his truck on a hill crashed into a house in the Brazilian city of Salvador—the same house he had crashed into 23 years earlier.

Housewife Cristina Costa said in a television interview outside her demolished home on Monday, "I opened the door and said, 'Not you again.'"

The driver declined to comment.

Ice Cream

REELSVILLE, IND. (UPI) A two-ton ice cream truck careened about 215 feet down a hill into a hickory tree with no one at the wheel but a nanny goat, state police said.

The driver, Donald D. Lee, 26, of Danville, Ill., stopped at a home to take an order Wednesday evening, leaving the door of his Schwan Ice Cream truck open and the parking brake engaged, said Trooper David L. Collins.

Collins said the goat ran from a barnyard, jumped into the truck cab and apparently disengaged the brake. The truck careened about 215 feet down a hill before it struck a hickory tree.

"The damage to the truck was over $5,000," Collins said. "It was pretty well totaled."

The goat was not injured.

Car

CHICKASHA, OKLA. (UPI) An elderly man who got out of his car to dump trash was run over three times by his own car Wednesday, the highway patrol said.

Curtis B. Hodson, 74, was in critical condition at Veterans Hospital in Oklahoma City.

Authorities said Hodson had stepped from his car to put trash in a dumpster. The car apparently was left in reverse with the engine running and a door open. The door knocked Hodson to the ground as the car moved past the first time.

The car went in a circle, running over him three times before a store manager stopped it, investigators said.

Business Is Business

Blind Haircutter

MIAMI (AP) Dave Melancon lost his sight in a 1986 home accident that should have ended his 10-year career as a hair stylist.

"But I'm headstrong and very independent," Melancon recalled at An Eye for Hair, the salon he opened in March.

Melancon, 40, was blinded after falling onto a metal sculpture he was making. But two former customers convinced him he could still cut hair.

"They called me and said nobody cut their hair like I had and wanted me to try," he said. "They came to my home and it came out all right."

Melancon won a $35,000 grant from the state to go into business. He has six sighted hairdressers working for him and about 10 regular customers for himself.

"I feel from the scalp to the end of the hair and listen to the scissors. My hearing and sense of touch are more acute now. I'm not scissor-happy," he said.

One customer, Robert Word, said "I kept promising him I'd let him cut my hair. He's such a nice guy. I finally gave in."

"I'm not scissor-happy."

"I called my regular barber and said, 'Don't you go anywhere. I'm having this blind guy cut my hair. When I'm finished, I want you to fix it,'" Word said.

But after Melancon was finished, Word said, he phoned his barber again to say, "I think I'm going to replace you."

Topless

DES MOINES, IOWA (UPI) The National Organization for Women says the new "Boob and Lube" garage with topless mechanics is sexploitation, but the owner likes their protests and says the publicity can only help his business.

"You're gonna make me rich," proprietor Darrel Lafon yelled to about 50 local NOW members carrying signs Tuesday in front of Darrel's Grease and Go near downtown Des Moines.

NOW says the topless "Boob and Lube" service the garage offers is a "shameless exploitation of women."

Lafon, who last month hired two women to vacuum and clean cars while topless, said business at his once-struggling garage has increased by more than 50 percent since the $24.88 topless service started.

NOW spokeswoman Jean Classon said Lafon has made money "by downgrading women."

"Nobody is saying it's not within the law," Classon said. 'We don't feel there are that many people who want to come to a business like this."

Lafon said he will continue to offer the optional topless service and added the publicity from the NOW protest will probably increase business.

Man Gets Phone Bill as Big as a Phone Book

HAMPTON, VIRGINIA (AP) Tugboat crewman Tom Scott knew the credit card call to his wife from New York via a marine-telephone linkup wouldn't be cheap.

But his bill, all 244 pages of it, totaled $11,178.84.

"I about fell on the floor," Scott said. "I couldn't believe it at first. It's thick as a telephone book. Then I realized what it was."

He had used his calling card, reading the number over the boat's radio to the marine operator.

"Evidently someone had some ears and picked up on it," he said.

Scott thinks whoever heard the number on the airwaves quickly sold it or allowed friends to use it. All the calls on the bill were from New York City, but they were to numbers as far away as Miami, Strasbourg, Missouri, and Mexico City.

"I about fell on the floor."

The AT&T security office called Scott right after it happened and asked if he used his card often, Scott said.

"I said, well, not really, maybe two or three times," he recalled. "They said like 48 times in one hour."

Scott said most of the calls were charged through National Telephone Service in Texas, which he said would get stuck with the bill.

Meantime, Scott says he will pay for one two-minute call, the original call to his wife from New York.

"That was about $4," he said.

Milk

HELSINKI (AFP) A breast-feeding mother who produced 300 liters (79 gallons) of excess milk over nine months has been awarded Finland's medal of merit, according to a reliable source here.

Lilja Virtanen, 28, from Jyvreskylae in central Finland, delivered her extra milk to a hospital, saving the lives of at least 20 premature babies.

She continues to breast-feed her two-year-old son and to sell her milk to the same hospital for five dollars a liter, tax-free, the source said.

Eternity in a Pub: O Death Where Is Thy Sting?

LONDON, ENGLAND (AP) A company has come up with the ultimate "last call" for people whose idea of heaven is a cozy English pub.

For $8,000, customers can have their ashes rest under their favorite stools or beneath the bar where they bent their elbows and be toasted every year as a not-quite-absent friend.

"Instead of being stuck in a cold graveyard in a cemetery where few people visit, the deceased will be surrounded by friends who will have a permanent reminder of the good times they enjoyed," says Colm O'Rourke, owner of the Little Pub Company.

Brewers Society spokesman Mike Ripley said he doubted anyone would ever be buried in a pub.

"It's a very silly story," Ripley said. "I suspect the idea was thought up at 11:55 on New Year's Eve and if someone had told me tomorrow was April First I wouldn't be at all surprised."

The Home Office, which regulates burials, said there were no regulations prohibiting ashes being buried in pubs—unless the corpse is already buried. Exhumations are not allowed.

The Little Pub Company is offering eternal rest at the Pack Horse, the Little Tumbling Sailor, or any of the other of its 10 pubs in western England, said the company's attorney, Jack Haywood.

Haywood describes O'Rourke as "an Irish millionaire who's completely barmy with these weird and wonderful pubs."

O'Rourke, 39, wants his ashes buried in the Pack Horse in his home village of Bewdley in Worcestershire, 95 miles northwest of London.

The plan was born, Haywood admitted, "when we'd had far too much to drink."

Dead customers could be accommodated anywhere in the pub, Haywood said. The fee would include an urn, a brass plaque and the annual wake.

"Why not give people the chance once they're cremated to be put in a block behind the bar as opposed to being scattered over a golf course?" he said. "I am going to be buried in one of our larger pubs, since I'm a big guy. Since my wife always finds me there, she will be used to visiting me there."

Coffins to Go

NEW WESTMINSTER, BRITISH COLUMBIA (Reuters) A retired Canadian Mountie, incensed by the high cost of dying, has opened a retail coffin store so you can pick a cut-price way to go.

Jack Turner, 55, says his Consumer Casket Center offers a better deal than funeral homes.

"It just suddenly dawned on me that the cost of dying was rather high. One of my reasons for opening was to give the consumer a better outlet, a better price for funeral merchandise because I thought the market to them was too restrictive," he said.

Turner, who reported that his business is slowly growing, said his best seller so far has been a $591 satin cottonwood coffin, which he claimed would cost twice as much if purchased through a funeral home.

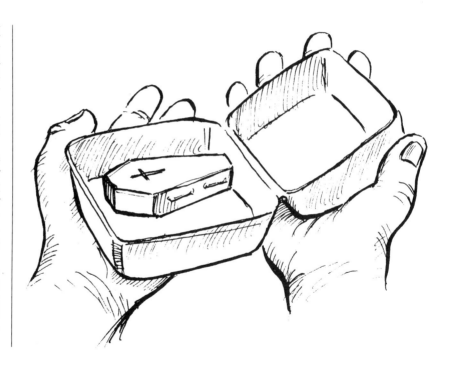

Honk If You're Grief-Stricken

WATERBURY, CONN. (AP) A Waterbury, Conn., funeral director is planning a funeral home with a drive-through window.

"The time has come for funeral homes to provide more convenient, accessible services," for busy people on the go, the funeral director, James Sanders, told AP.

So the coffin will be displayed in a drive-through window during the day and moved inside the funeral home for a more traditional wake in the evening.

The drive-through will even have a slot where visitors paying their respects may leave cards.

Sanders said that while drive-in viewing windows are fairly common on the West Coast, there are none in New England.

Birds Do It, Bees Do It

Lonely Deer Finds Company with Concrete Yard Animals

ARENZVILLE, ILLINOIS (UPI) A lonely and confused deer mistook two concrete lawn ornaments for the real thing recently, making love to them for several hours before giving up his amorous pursuits.

The episode took place at Jim Kloker's farm in west-central Illinois. Kloker said the buck emerged from the woods and charged the concrete buck on his front lawn.

"Of course, he didn't hit it because the concrete didn't charge back, but then he turned and mounted the concrete doe and made love to it," Kloker said. "Then he made love to both of them for about three hours."

Kloker tried to scare the young buck away by shouting at it but nothing seemed to break the deer's concentration.

"I grabbed my rifle and went out to shoot it but I just couldn't do it," he said. "Hell, he thought they were real deer."

He said the buck rested on the ground after each rendezvous, gained

his strength and went back to work.

The deer finally was scared away when a truck drove by, but not before Kloker photographed the incident.

Kloker said the experience took its toll on the yard doe as its tail broke off during one of the young buck's romantic interludes. The concrete buck, however, survived the episode intact.

Elephant Dies of Stress

COPENHAGEN, DENMARK (AP) Frederik the elephant, who had been pestered for years by seven aggressive she-elephants, has died of a heart attack brought on by stress, his keeper said Friday.

"It was as if he'd given up hope for a decent life..."

"It was as if he'd given up hope for a decent life after the rough treatment he suffered at the hands of his wives recently," said Leif Nielsen, director of the Givskud Lion Park zoo in Jutland, west Denmark.

Nielsen said that on Monday three of the female elephants with whom Frederik had shared a yard for years ganged up on him and shoved him into a pond.

"Frederik had always been a bit frail," said Nielsen. "He couldn't fend for himself and never recovered from his bout in the pond."

The 16-year-old, three-ton elephant had to be lifted from the water with a crane. Two veterinarians worked for four days to save Frederik's life, but the pachyderm died Thursday.

Every time Frederik tried to turn his amorous attentions to one female, the others would mob him out of jealousy, and Nielsen.

The zoo is considering acquiring a new, more robust male elephant who can cope with the females and sire offspring.

Farmer Shoots Moose that Had Hung Around His Horses

NEWBURGH, MAINE (AP) A farmer shot a lonesome moose that had been keeping vigil near four mares on his farm in this central Maine town, saying the wild animal had spooked his horses.

John Calderwood said today he shot the female moose, which first appeared at his Burnt Swamp Farm on Feb. 16, during a driving snowstorm Wednesday night.

He said he earlier received permission from a game warden to kill the moose if it threatened his horses. It is illegal to shoot moose in Maine except during the six-day hunting season in October.

Calderwood said one of his 16 horses lost nearly 100 pounds and four others also lost weight while the moose was hanging around. He attributed the weight loss to fear of the moose.

"I'm sure that this moose was looking for companionship" and its presence "wasn't a big problem at any one time," Calderwood said in a telephone interview from his home.

One of his 16 horses lost nearly 100 pounds... [for] fear of the moose.

"But every time the moose came back, it became more threatening," he said. The horses didn't "like it at all, probably the smells. I don't know what all."

No charges have been filed against Calderwood, pending completion of an investigation, according to the state Warden Service.

Calderwood said he's gotten a number of critical calls about the shooting.

The calls were "real profane, mostly from women," he said. "It was terrible. And a couple of them threatened our farm and our horses."

Calderwood said he has raised horses for sale and show at his 50-acre farm for 12 years.

Love Is Just a Four-legged Word

HARARE, ZIMBABWE (AFP) A 59-year-old Zimbabwean who was caught having sex with a cow has been jailed for three months and told by a judge to try prostitutes instead, the *Herald* reported Tuesday.

Charles Chakomera, who was caught in the act by the farmer, was warned he would face a long sentence if he did it again. He pleaded guilty.

Pelican

ATHENS (AFP) Four thousand people on the Greek Aegean Sea island of Gyros today stormed the local court to lynch a 28-year-old Moroccan dishwasher who pleaded guilty to the rape-murder of a pelican.

He was also accused of attempting to rape two German women tourists.

The court was told that Abdelbrim Taltal, a married man with a child, had raped "Marcos the Pelican" on the nearby island of Timos.

The pelican was the island mascot.

Police said that Taltal's clothing and underwear bore the traces of the pelican's feathers.

Brothel with a Difference Busted in Paris

PARIS, FRANCE (Reuters) A brothel employing bored housewives, well-paid businesswomen and even a 73-year-old grandmother has been busted by police in a respectable Paris neighborhood.

The brothel keeper, "Madame Marcelle," was a 65-year-old woman seeking distraction after the death of her husband, Vice Squad Inspector Jean-Pierre Gambini said.

He said her 20 or so prostitutes were mainly highly respectable women who charged $100 for their favors in Madame Marcelle's central Paris apartment, a fraction of the going rate. The only professional among the 20 prostitutes working for Madame Marcelle was 73-year-old "Huguette," who had set up her own brothel 30 years ago and was arrested then.

She told police she had joined the Paris brothel, despite her advanced years, out of nostalgia for her old job.

Stadium Sex Leads to New Rules at Toronto Hotel

TORONTO (Reuters) A couple who made love in a hotel room in full sight of a packed baseball stadium have forced the hotel to warn guests they can be seen by the crowd.

The SkyDome Hotel, built inside Toronto's new stadium, has 70 rooms that give a direct view of the playing field. The couple's sexual performance was a highlight of Tuesday's game between the local Blue Jays and the Seattle Mariners.

"There isn't a more exciting way to watch a baseball game, but for some people it's more exciting than others," hotel manager Ray Thompson said on Thursday.

"What our guests do behind closed doors is their own business, as long as it's not criminal and there's no damage. But when there are witnesses, the guests are subject to immediate eviction and possible criminal charges."

In an earlier incident a guest committed an indecent act in full view of the crowd in the belief that the bedroom window was one-way glass.

The hotel now plans to ask guests to sign an official waiver when they occupy rooms overlooking the field.

Crowds Flocking To See Moose Courting A Cow

SHREWSBURY, VT (UPI) Thousands of people have been stopping at a central Vermont farm to see a moose try to woo an unwilling cow, the cow's owner said today.

"It's like the World's Fair," said Larry Carrara, the owner of the Hereford cow. He said the crowds have not deterred the confused moose.

Since last week, visitors have come from around the country to see the moose. The local authorities estimate Saturday's crowd at 4,000 people.

Most of the time the animals merely stand near each other, Mr. Carrara said, but the moose has made attempts at physical contact, only to be rebuffed as the cow fled.

Wildlife experts say cross-species courtships often occur in the mating season, but are extremely unlikely to result in offspring.

Mr. Carrara said he expected the moose to give up his pursuit within a week.

Asked why the moose was so enamored, the farmer said, "After all, she is very good looking."

Lovemakers Delay Orient Express

INNSBRUCK, AUSTRIA (Reuters) A couple making love on the Paris-to-Venice "Orient Express" delayed the luxury train for 40 minutes at Innsbruck yesterday when the woman's foot jammed the emergency brake, railway officials said today.

Engineers surprised the couple in their compartment after searching the carriages to discover why the train's brakes were locked at the station. The express later continued to Venice.

About the Authors

MONICA HOOSE was born in Berlin but has lived in Washington, D.C., for most of her life. She earned an M.A. from Northwestern University's Medill School of Journalism and is a producer for the award-winning MacNeil/Lehrer NewsHour.

CAROLYN NAIFEH was born in Tulsa, Oklahoma, but lived abroad as a diplomat's brat—in the Mideast, Africa, and South Asia—until college. She earned an M.A. in Latin American Studies from Vanderbilt University and is a reporter for the Voice of America.